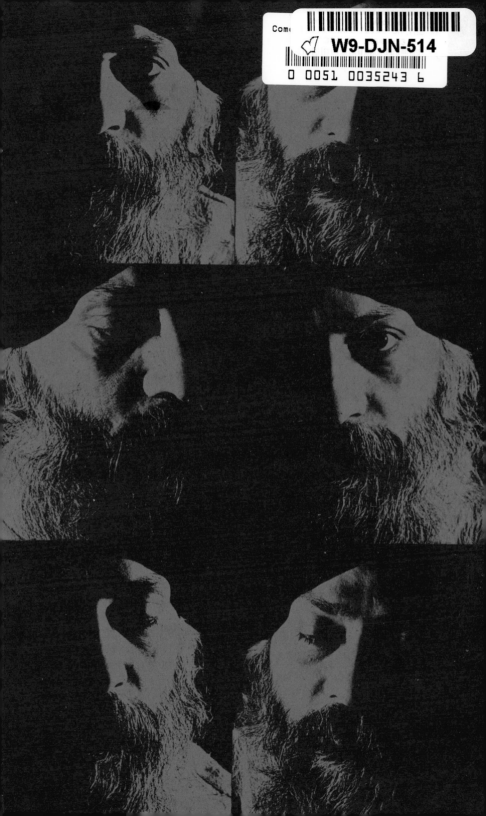

COME, FOLLOW ME

Volume 3

Come follow me

VOLUME THREE

Bhagwan Shree Rajneesh

talks on the sayings of Jesus

RAJNEESH  FOUNDATION

Copyright 1976 by Rajneesh Foundation.

First Edition:

Published by:

Ma Yoga Laxmi
Rajneesh Foundation
Shree Rajneesh Ashram, 17 Koregaon Park
Poona 411 001, Maharashtra, India

Printed by:

Vakil & Sons Ltd.
Vakils House
18, Ballard Estate
Bombay 400 038

On paper supplied by Chimanlals

Printed in India

CONTENTS

COME, FOLLOW ME   Volume 3

This is the third in a series of four volumes of discourses by
Bhagwan Shree Rajneesh on the Life of Jesus.

These ten discourses, given at the ashram in Poona from
eleventh to twentieth December 1975, are based on excerpts
taken from the Gospels of Matthew and John in the authorized
King James version of the Bible.

Compilation and Editing   Swami Deva Paritosh

Coordination   Ma Ananda Vandana

Design   Swami Prem Deekshant

INTRODUCTION

"... I am drunk with Jesus. Jesus is a wine; he is not a man, he is an intoxication. And once you have tasted of him, nothing of this world will be meaningful to you. .... When I talk about Jesus, you feel I am bringing a new breeze to you—because I am not a missionary, I am not a Christian, I am not a priest. In fact I have nothing to do with Jesus except that I love him. .... There is only one way to see Jesus, and that is to see him as he is, directly. No scriptures are needed to interpret him; he has to be seen untranslated; he has to be seen direct. .... Jesus or a Buddha are like a honey-bee. The honey-bee goes and finds beautiful flowers in a valley. She comes back; she dances a dance of ecstasy near her friends to tell them she has found a beautiful valley full of flowers. Come, follow me. A Jesus is just a honey-bee who has found the original source of life, a valley of beautiful flowers, flowers of eternity. He comes and dances near you to give you the message: Come, follow me."

I have chosen at random the above excerpts from the discourses contained in this volume. Jesus comes alive for us in a new and startling way—not the Jesus that the theologians and the scholars have presented to us. "... Jesus has been taught from a thousand and one pulpits. .... More books are written on Jesus than on anybody else. More churches stand in his name than in anybody else's name ... and I tell you, Jesus is one of the most unknown Masters."

So here is this Master in India recognizing with love the Master Jesus, and communicating him to us in this twentieth century with understanding and deep insight, and supreme authority.

> *If any man thirst,*
> *let him come unto me and drink.*

"Jesus is water of eternity, a divine well. He can quench your thirst. . . ."

Then Bhagwan makes the seemingly astonishing statement— "If any man thirst, let him come unto me and drink, because yet a little while more am I with you. And then I go unto him that sent me. . . . Seek your thirst. If you are thirsty, then I am ready to become a well for you. The thirst can disappear, and only when your thirst disappears, for the first time you will feel what life is and its meaning—the beauty of it, the glory of it."

I was fortunate to arrive in Poona just in time to listen to these sublime discourses. And the lovers of Jesus, and those coming to him for the first time, are privileged to have these discourses available now, to be read with delight. So, drink and enjoy.

Swami Deva Paritosh

54 And when he was come into his own country,
   he taught them in their synagogue,
   insomuch that they were astonished, and said,
   Whence hath this man this wisdom,
   and these mighty works?

55 Is not this the carpenter's son?
   is not his mother called Mary?
   and his brethren, James,
   and Joses, and Simon, and Judas?

56 And his sisters, are they not all with us?
   Whence then hath this man all these things?

57 And they were offended in him.
   But Jesus said unto them,
   A prophet is not without honour,
   save in his own country,
   and in his own house.

MATTHEW 14

22 . . . Jesus constrained his disciples
   to get into a ship,
   and to go before him unto the other side . . .

23 And . . . he went up into a mountain
   apart to pray:
   and when the evening was come,
   he was there alone.

24 But the ship
   was now in the midst of the sea,
   tossed with waves:
   for the wind was contrary.

25 And in the fourth watch of the night
    Jesus went unto them,
    walking on the sea.

26 And when the disciples saw him
    walking on the sea,
    they were troubled, saying,
    It is a spirit;
    and they cried out for fear.

27 But straightway
    Jesus spake unto them, saying,
    Be of good cheer; it is I;
    be not afraid.

28 And Peter answered him and said,
    Lord, if it be thou,
    bid me come unto thee on the water.

29 And he said, Come.
    And when Peter was come down
    out of the ship,
    he walked on the water,
    to go to Jesus.

30 But when he saw the wind boisterous,
    he was afraid;
    and beginning to sink, he cried, saying,
    Lord, save me.

31 And immediately
    Jesus stretched forth his hand,
    and caught him, and said unto him,
    O thou of little faith,
    wherefore didst thou doubt?

1 Jesus is like a wilderness: raw, but alive, rebellious.

I AM A DRUNKARD. You may believe it or not, but I am a drunkard. You can look into my eyes and you can see it—I am drunk with Jesus. And Jesus is a wine; he is not a man, he's an intoxication. And once you have tasted of him, then nothing of this world will ever be meaningful to you. Once the meaning from the beyond enters into your life, this whole world becomes futile, immaterial, insignificant.

Religion is a sort of intoxication. This has to be understood because without a deep intoxication, your life will never have any meaning. It will remain superficial prose and will never become a poem. You will walk but you will never be able to dance, and unless you dance you have missed. Unless you dance with such abundance, with such forgetfulness that you disappear in it, that the dancer is lost and only the dance remains . . . only then. And only then will you be able to know what life is.

I remember: Once Alexander the Great asked Diogenes, "You are so learned, you know so much. Can't you tell me something about God, what God is?"

Diogenes waited for a moment and then said, "Give me one day's time."

Alexander came the next day but again Diogenes said, "Give me two days' time." And it happened again, and he said, "Give me three days' time," and then four days and then five days, and then six days and the whole week was gone.

Alexander was annoyed and said, "What do you mean? If you don't know the answer you should have told me before. If you know, then what is the explanation for the delay?"

Diogenes said, "That moment you asked me, I thought that I knew. But the more I tried to catch hold of it, the more it became elusive. The more I thought about it, the farther away it was. Right now, I don't know anything, and the only thing I can say to you," said Diogenes, "is that those who think they know God, they know not."

God can be known only when you are not. This is the meaning when I say, "Until you become a drunkard"—so that your ego is lost. I am a drunkard, drunk with Jesus. And when I will be talking to you about Jesus, it is not about Jesus. I am not a theologian, not a Christian, not a scholar. Theologians talk 'about', they go round and round, they beat around the bush. I am not going to talk about Jesus, I am going to talk Jesus. And when I talk about Jesus, it is not that I am talking about him, rather, he talks himself. I give him way, I become a passage. All that I do is that I don't hinder him. That is the only way to talk about Jesus or Buddha or Krishna. And when I will be talking Jesus I will not talk about Christ. Jesus is real, Christ is a principle. Jesus is concrete, Christ is abstract. Jesus is a man like you and me, of blood and bone. His heart beats. He laughs, he cries, he loves, he lives.

Christ is a dead concept, bloodless; there is no heart beating there. Christianity is concerned with Christ, I am not concerned with Christ. The word 'Christ' is beautiful, but corrupted, contaminated, polluted. The whole beauty of it has been destroyed.

Whenever a word is used by theologians it loses meaning and purity and innocence—then it is no more virgin. Jesus is still virgin, Christ is corrupted. Christ is a concept, Jesus is reality, concrete reality.

*L*ook! I love human beings, but not humanity. Humanity does not exist. Only concrete human beings exist—someone here, someone there, but it is always someone. Humanity is an empty word. And just like that is Christ. Jesus exists, sometimes in Gautam the Buddha, sometimes in Mohammed the prophet, sometimes in Krishna the fluteplayer—somewhere here, somewhere there, but it is always a concrete phenomenon. Christ is abstract. It exists only in the books of philosophy and theology. Christ has never walked on the earth. Or, we can say it another way: Christ is the son of God, Jesus the son of man.

Let me talk about Jesus the son of man, because only the son of man is real, and only the son of man can grow and become the son of God. Only man can grow and become God, because man is the seed, the source; God is the flowering. God does not exist anywhere. When you flower, God comes into existence—it comes into existence and disappears . . . it comes into existence and disappears. When Buddha was here, God existed. When Jesus was here, God existed. When Jesus disappears, God disappears—just as when a flower disappears, it disappears. God is not somewhere, always existing, otherwise God will never be fresh and young—it will gather too much dust, it will become dirty. It comes into existence whenever a man realises his sins, whenever a man really exists. Whenever a man exists in totality, God exists in those rare moments. So when you come and ask me, "Where is God?" I cannot show you. Unless you have proof of him in your own being, he will not be there. Until you become him he is not. Everybody has to realise him in his own innermost shrine, in his own being. You carry him as a seed.

It is up to you to allow it to grow and become a great tree.

So I will not be talking about Christ, but about Jesus. Let Christ be imprisoned in the churches—that is the right place for Christ to exist. I would like Jesus to enter your hearts. Forget Christ, remember Jesus. But just the opposite has happened. People have forgotten Jesus and their minds have been hammered continuously for two thousand years, hammered to remember Christ. Christ cannot transform you, because there exists no bridge between you and Christ. Then there exists an unbridgeable abyss. But with Jesus you are close. You can call Jesus 'brother', but you cannot call Christ 'brother'. And until you feel a deep brotherhood, a bridge, how can Jesus be of any help to you? Jesus is tremendously beautiful—his beauty has a dimension of its own. Buddha is beautiful, but Jesus is totally different from Buddha. In Buddha a different type of silence was incarnated.

I have heard about a Chinese emperor. He had two great painters in his court, and there was always rivalry. They were always fighting and competing, and it was almost impossible to decide who was the greater. Both were masters of their art. One day the emperor said, "Now you do one thing: you both paint on one theme so that it can be decided who is the greater, and the theme is 'Rest'." The first painter, of course, chose a very obvious subject: he painted a very silent lake, far away in the mountains, lone, still, not even a ripple on the surface. Just looking at that painting you would feel sleepy. The other painter tried something absolutely opposite: he painted a thundering waterfall . . . for miles the white foam of it . . . and just near the waterfall a very fragile, delicate birch tree, the branches bowing down, touching the foam, and on the birch the small nest of a robin, and the robin sitting on the nest, with closed eyes, almost wet.

The first is a non-dynamic silence: more like death, less like life. The opposite doesn't exist in it. The rest has no tension in it; the 'rest' is more like absence than like presence. The second is a dynamic concept: 'rest', but not dead. It is alive, throbbing. The thunder, the waterfall, the tremendous activity, and the nest, and the robin sitting there, silent. . . .

Jesus is like the second painting, Buddha comes closer to the first painting. Of course it is very silent, but the opposite is missing—and without the opposite, music cannot be created. Buddha has a single note, he is not an orchestra. Jesus has opposite notes meeting, merging and creating a harmony, a symphony. Buddha is silent, without revolution. Jesus is silent, with a deep rebellion around him. This has to be remembered. Only then you will understand how to penetrate into his very heart. Why did Jesus become so significant, why did he appeal to so many people all through these centuries?—he has something of the wild in him. He is not a garden, he is a wilderness. He is raw, not refined. You touch him and you will know. You feel him and you will know. Buddha is very cultured, very refined. He has something of the court of a king. Jesus comes from a village, a carpenter's son, uneducated, uncultured. He is like a wilderness: raw, but alive, rebellious. Hence, the appeal; hence he has touched millions of people's hearts. You can understand him. He is more than you but you are in him. You cannot understand Buddha. He is more than you but you are not there. With Jesus a bridge exists.

Now these sutras.

> *And when he was come into his own country,*
> *he taught them in their synagogue,*
> *insomuch that they were astonished, and said,*
> *Whence hath this man this wisdom*
> *and these mighty works?*
>
> *Is not this the carpenter's son?*

is not his mother called Mary?
and his brethren, James,
and Joses, and Simon, and Judas?

And his sisters, are they not all with us?
Whence then hath this man all these things?

And they were offended in him.

Nobody was so much offended in Buddha, ever; nobody was so much offended in Lao Tzu, ever; nobody was offended, as people were offended with Jesus. Why? A Buddha is a faraway peak. If you cannot understand him, how can you be offended with him? If you cannot understand him, how can you argue with him?—he is so far away, so beyond. At the most, all you can do is to worship him. So Buddha was worshipped and Jesus crucified. Wherever Buddha moved nobody was offended in him. Either people could not understand him—but then you could not be offended—or people could understand him, but then they understood that he was the very essence of the Upanishads, the very incarnation of the Vedas. He is all essential tradition. There was no question of being offended in him.

With Jesus people were offended, he was just like them. They could not understand him. They said, "Is not this the carpenter's son?" Buddha was a son of a great emperor, Mahavir also, Krishna also, Ram also. All the great Indian incarnations came from royal families. Jesus is the first man who comes from a poor house. Nobody had ever known him. And if Jesus had not been born, nobody would ever have heard about the family. Buddha was already established with the family name, with a long tradition and heritage, a long lineage of prestige and power. Jesus comes from a powerless poor family, almost a beggar. People could not understand—"From where comes his power? From where comes this wisdom? Is not this the carpenter's son? Is not his mother called Mary?" The people wondered—"He belongs to us and talks about God. He belongs to us and says, 'I am the son of God.' He belongs to us, he was working in his father's workshop and suddenly, what has happened to him?" They were offended in him, the ego was offended.

Buddha was always great. Even if he had not become enlightened, he would have been worshipped like an emperor. People had always touched his feet. He was always great and beyond them. When he moved amidst the people and renounced his kingdom, he became even greater because he had renounced his kingdom. People can understand the language of money and they cannot understand any other language. They worship you if you have money, they worship you if you renounce money. But they understand only one language—the language of money. If you don't have anything, they don't bother about you. And if you don't have anything how can you renounce, what can you renounce?

This is one of the most important things to understand about the Indian mind, the so-called Indian religious mind. Even that mind can understand only the language of money. Mahavir renounced. The Jain scriptures go on relating how much he renounced: how many elephants, how many horses, how many chariots, how much gold, how many diamonds. They go on and on and on. Why? Why have these accounts been kept? And the reality is that he was never a very great king. The kingdom was very small, not more than a small district. And his father was not more than a collector of a district, not more than that. Because in Mahavir's time India was divided into two thousand kingdoms, so it could not be very great. And it is almost impossible that he had so many elephants and so many chariots and so much gold, it is exaggeration. But people understand only the language of money. They exaggerate, because that is the only way to prove that Mahavir was very great. Had he been the son of a carpenter, nobody would have ever bothered about him.

Jesus is a revolution in the world of religion. He is the first
poor man who declared, "I am the son of God." He is the first
poor man who dared to declare, "I am a prophet, a teerthankera,
an avatar." Never before had such a thing happened in the
history of man. He opened the way for many others to follow.
Then Mohammed could declare, and then came Kabir, and
Sena, and Nanak, and Dadu, and many more. Jesus opened the
gate—that even a poor man who had nothing to renounce, can
renounce, because the real renunciation is not of wealth, but
of the ego. The real renunciation is not of wealth, let me repeat
it, but of the ego. It is not a question of renouncing what you
have, it is a question of renouncing what you are. You can have
much and you can renounce that. But if the ego continues—
and it can continue—it can be fulfilled by having much, it can
be fulfilled by renouncing much. And if the ego is there, you
remain ordinary, you remain superficial.

And they were offended in him. Had he been an emperor's son,
they would have fallen at his feet. But he was just an ordinary
carpenter's son and everybody in the village knew about him.

> *But Jesus said unto them,*
> *A prophet is not without honour,*
> *save in his own country,*
> *and in his own house.*

A great insight. Why has it happened so many times, that
people who are closest always misunderstand? We should have
expected just the contrary, that the people of Jesus' village would
understand him first. Before anyone else would understand him,
the people of Jesus' house, family, relatives, would understand
him first. But it doesn't happen. Why? A deep insight into the
human ego is needed to understand it. With those who are
close to you, it is very difficult to believe that they had gone
beyond and above you. If somebody else who is not close to
you goes beyond you, maybe you are not bothered—he is so

far away, the competitive ego does not arise. But if your own brother goes and you are left behind—and you were born to the same parents, you lived in the same house, and you were educated in the same school; and your own brother goes so far away—your ego is hurt. Then what have you been doing? You feel defeated, you feel a loser. Then the easiest way is to deny that he has gone beyond, then the easiest way is to prove that he is just as ordinary as you are ordinary. The easiest way is to disprove his claim, to deny.

 A prophet is not without honour, save in his own country, and in his own house. I would like to add one thing more: "And in his own time."

 You worship Buddha now, very easily. No problem arises because there is a distance of twenty-five centuries. You worship Mahavir. All over the world millions go on praying to Jesus. These same people crucified him. They are the same people who were offended in him, who denied him. What has happened?—a distance of two thousand years. Now, your ego doesn't feel offended, you don't have any competition with him; maybe he was really a son of God. But he offended his own contemporaries. He was talking one day in a village and somebody asked "Do you believe in Abraham, the founder of Judaism?" Jesus said something which has been offending Jews since then. Jesus said, "Abraham? Before Abraham was, I am." Let me repeat it in another way: if Christians come to me and ask, "Do you believe in Jesus?" and I tell them, "Before Jesus was, I am," they will be offended. They will never be able to forgive me.

 This man Jesus is claiming that he is someone who was, even before Abraham. They had known that he was born in their village, they knew his birth date, they knew his father and his mother and his sisters and his brothers. They were still working in their workshop and this man said, "I am, before Abraham was." This was going too far—"No, he cannot be forgiven for it." But what he was saying was the truth, because Jesus is a

quality, which has nothing to do with any person. It is a quality
like love. If you say, "Before Abraham was, love is," nobody
will be offended because love is not a person. You don't take it
as a person, you take it as a quality. Jesus is a quality of tremendous love. Jesus is a quality of tremendous perception, vision, of
tremendous realisation. Jesus is a quality—but to see that quality
you will have to drop your egos. Only then can you see, otherwise your egos will be heavy on your eyes and it will be almost
impossible to see.

*J*ust a few days ago, I was reading G. K. Chesterton's life.
He lived his whole life in London. One day he was pre-
paring for a journey, a long journey, and everything was
packed, everything was ready. A friend asked, "Where are
you going?" Chesterton said, "I am going to London." The
friend said, "Your wit, your remark escapes me. What do you
mean? We *are* in London, so where are you going?" Chesterton
said, "I am going to London via Paris, via Bombay, via Tokyo,
via New York, because I have lived in London so long that
my eyes have become clouded and I cannot see where London
is, what London is."

When Jesus is standing just in front of you, you cannot see
him. You will have to go via—via the Vatican, via Rome, via
popes and preachers and churches. Only then may you be able
to see who Jesus is. When Jesus confronts you, he offends. His
very being, his height, his depth, become offensive. You feel
that you have failed. You feel that you have not lived. You feel
that you have not loved. You will become an enemy. With
Jesus these are the two possibilities: either you follow him or you
become the enemy. You cannot remain neutral, you cannot remain indifferent. Either you follow him if you can drop the
ego—then you take a jump, you flow with him; or, if you are
defensive, you become the enemy, you become the foe and you

start destroying him. Because his very presence is offensive, he
has to be destroyed.

When Jesus was crucified, a great weight disappeared from the
Jewish mind. You felt relieved. He was somebody who was a
constant reminder that you were failures, somebody who was
a constant reminder that you had not lived, somebody who
was a constant reminder that you were empty, hollow within,
that you were not fulfilled. Contemporaries cannot understand.
Very rare people, rare because they can drop their egos, can see
what Jesus is. And even their vision is always shaking, even
their vision is not very certain, even their vision has deep hesita-
tion and doubt in it. Even those who follow, follow with much
doubt in them.

> *. . . Jesus constrained his disciples*
> *to get into a ship,*
> *and to go before him unto the other side . . .*

> *And . . . he went up into a mountain apart to pray.*

That was always a practice with him that whenever he would
move into the multitudes, into the crowd, afterwards he would
go alone into deep prayer and meditation. Why? If you have
been meditating you will understand. Those who have been
meditating with me, they will understand that once you start
meditating, a very fragile quality, a very delicate quality of
consciousness is born in you. A flower of the unknown starts
opening—it is delicate. And whenever you go into the crowd
you lose something. Whenever you come back home from the
crowd, you come lesser than you had gone. Something has been
lost, some contact has been broken. The crowd pulls you down,
it has a gravitation of its own.

You may not feel it if you live on the same plane. Then there
is no problem, then you have nothing to lose. In fact, when you
live in the crowd, with the crowd, on the same plane, alone you

feel very uneasy. Whenever you are with people you feel very good and happy. Your aloneness becomes sad, your aloneness is not aloneness, it is a loneliness; you miss the other. You don't find yourself in it, you simply miss the other. When you are alone, you are not alone, because you are not there. Only that desire to be with others is there—that is what loneliness is. Always remember the distinction between aloneness and loneliness. Aloneness is a peak of experience. Loneliness is a valley. Aloneness has light in it, a flame. Loneliness is dark and damp. Loneliness is when you desire others; aloneness is when you enjoy yourself.

Whenever Jesus would move into the multitudes, into the crowd, and particularly when he came to his own town, he would tell his disciples to go to the other shore of the lake, and he would move into total aloneness. Not even disciples were allowed to be with him. This was a constant practice with him, he knew the art. Whenever you go into the crowd you are infected by it. You need a higher altitude to purify yourself, you need to be alone so that you can become fresh again. You need to be alone with yourself, so that you become together again, so that you again become centred, rooted. Whenever you move with others, they push you off centre.

> *And . . . he went up into a mountain*
> *apart to pray:*
> *and when the evening was come,*
> *he was there alone.*

Nothing is said about his prayer, what he did there, just the word 'pray'. There is no prayer mentioned. To be in a prayerful mood is enough. When you say something it is not prayer. Before God or before existence, you need simply to be vulnerable —that is prayer. You are not to say something. On the contrary, you have to listen—what does existence want to say to you? So whenever you go to pray, don't start saying something. God already knows what you are going to say. It is foolish, it is ridiculous. And what can you say, what do you have to say? It will be all nonsense. It will all be nothing but desires, demands, and deep down, complaints. And a prayer with complaints is no prayer, a prayer with deep gratitude is prayer. There is no need to say anything, you can just be silent. A prayer is not talking, it is listening.

Hence nothing is said about what Jesus did in his aloneness. It simply says 'apart to pray'. He went apart, he became alone. That is what prayer is, to be alone, where the other is not felt; where the other is not standing between you and existence, where you are vulnerable, open; when God's breeze can pass through you, unhindered. It is a cleansing experience. It rejuvenates your spirit. It takes away all the dust that ordinarily gathers around. To be with God simply means to be alone. You can miss the point—if you start thinking about God, then you are not alone. If you start talking to God, then in your imagination you have created the other. And then your God is doing nothing; he is just a projection. In that projection you will find all the others that you have ever known: your father will be there—whenever you say to God, "Father," your father will be there, a part of you projected. Or you say, "Mother," your mother will be there. All words are your words, so whatsoever you say will be your projection. A prayer is not to say anything. It is to be simply silent, open, ready to listen—it is a listening. And there is no need to believe in God because that too is a projection. The only need is to be alone, to be capable of being alone—and immediately, you are with God. Whenever you are alone, you are with God. To say 'with God' is not exactly right because that shows that you are here and God is there. It would be better to say that whenever you are alone, God is, and you are not, and there is prayer.

Prayer is a fragrance that arises whenever you are ready to be alone. Whenever you are not afraid to be alone, it arises. Some-

thing opens within you like a lotus, and that lotus is in tune with
the whole around you. You dissolve, you meet and merge,
boundaries disappear. You are no more an island, you have become part of the continent. God is, you are not.

> *And . . . he went up into a mountain*
> *apart to pray:*
> *and when the evening was come,*
> *he was there alone.*

Why not before? Because to be alone needs much preparation . . .
he must have been throwing away all the impressions that he
had gathered from the multitude and the crowd the whole
day . . . he was throwing away those impressions . . . the dust . . .
by the evening he was alone, by the evening he came to a point
where no thought stirred; he came to a point when the flame of
consciousness was there without any smoke. By the evening he
became centred, by the evening he went into a deep rest within
himself—he returned home.

> *But the ship*
> *was now in the midst of the sea,*
> *tossed with the waves:*
> *for the wind was contrary*

. . . and the disciples were going to the other shore.
   "And the ship was in the midst of the sea, tossed with the
waves, for the wind was contrary." This is a parable. Jesus is alone,
or, Jesus is with his God. Jesus is beyond time and space, but
the disciples are crossing from this shore to the other shore.
The other shore means the God, the beyond.

> *But the ship*
> *was now in the midst of the sea,*
> *tossed with the waves:*
> *for the wind was contrary.*

And the wind is always contrary in the world, and the sea is always troubled, because it is a sea of desires, because it is a sea of ignorance. And the wind is always contrary because it is a sea of competitiveness and jealousies and hatred, of violence and aggression—the wind is always contrary. Jesus is beyond, alone, centred; but his disciples are struggling towards the other shore.

> *And in the fourth watch of the night*
> *Jesus went unto them,*
> *walking on the sea.*

It is a beautiful parable. Christians have completely missed the point of it, because they think it is a historical fact, they think that Jesus really walked on water. He was not a magician. He was a simple man. And this is a parable, not a historical event. Because of Christians, even Jesus looks ridiculous; he has fallen into bad company.

And in the fourth watch of the night . . . What is the meaning of the fourth watch of the night?—when the night is darkest, when the night has the most abysmal depth in it, the darkest part of it. The master can help the disciple only when the disciple reaches the fourth part of the night, the darkest part. That darkest part has always been known by the mystics as the dark night of the soul. Jesus was trained by certain mystics who were called Essenes. They say that on everybody's pilgrimage towards God, there comes a point when one has to pass through the darkest hour of the night: the dark night of the soul. And in the fourth watch of the night, the darkest part, Jesus went unto them.

You can call your master for help only when you have done all that can be done. If you are lazy, and if you have not done anything, the master's help is impossible. Help becomes possible only when you have come to the darkest hour of your night beyond which you cannot do anything else; where you feel totally helpless, when you hang between life and death—only

then is help possible. When you are helpless, only then is help
possible. If you go on thinking that you can still help yourself,
or that life is still in your control, then the master is not needed.
Only at a certain stage, when you feel yourself absolutely incapable of doing anything—you are simply in chaos, all control
lost, helpless, totally helpless—only then the master's help becomes possible.

> *And in the fourth watch of the night*
> *Jesus went unto them,*
> *walking on the sea.*

And of course Jesus walks on the sea, the sea of desires, the sea of
ignorance, the sea of the egos. In the East we understand the
parable. One of the greatest masters of Zen, Lin-chi, has said,
"Walk, but don't allow your feet to be touched by the water."
One has to live in the world, but not be of the world—one has
to walk on the world. Jesus is not an escapist, he's not running
from the world. He walks on the sea, he lives in the midst of the
world, but he does not allow the water to touch his feet. This
is what in the East we call 'to live like a lotus'. It lives in the water
but the water cannot touch it—even the dewdrops may settle on
it, but they never touch it, there remains a gap. To become a lotus
flower—that is the meaning of this parable.

> *And in the fourth watch of the night*
> *Jesus went unto them,*
> *walking on the sea.*

It is a parable of the inner turmoil of man, of the inner chaos
of man, of the inner contrary wind, of the inner struggle to go
to the other shore. It has nothing to do with the lake of Galilee.
These things are of the inner world—they are not events
that have happened outside, they are processes of inner
growth.

And when the disciples saw him
walking on the sea,
they were troubled, saying,
It is a spirit;
and they cried out for fear.

This is my experience also; many times it has happened. This is why I say that this is a parable. Somebody who is working deeply with me, growing, is in some dark night of the soul. He needs my help, and I go to him and he trembles, and he becomes afraid. Many times I say to my disciples, "If I come, don't get scared." At that time they laugh, they think I am joking. But when I reach them they tremble and they cannot believe that I have come. They can believe anything, but they cannot believe that I have come, because that is beyond their scope.

And when the disciples saw him
walking on the sea,
they were troubled, saying,
It is a spirit; a ghost.

How can Jesus walk on the sea? It must be a ghost.

. . . and they cried out for fear.

Even with your master, you are related with fear, not with love, because love believes and fear disbelieves. Love is trust, fear is distrust. In that moment the disciples showed that their trust was just on the surface. If Jesus comes in the inner world, they cannot believe, they cannot trust.

. . . they cried out for fear.

But straightway
Jesus spake unto them, saying,
Be of good cheer; it is I;
be not afraid.

It is I, be not afraid. Be of good cheer. But you have forgotten how to be cheerful, you have forgotten how to be blissful, you have forgotten the taste of happiness. You know only agony, you know only anguish, you understand only hell. Heaven looks like a dream, a utopia, so that exists in your hopes, but it is not a reality.

Jesus said, "Be of good cheer! Be happy! I have come to you. And you are crying out for fear! Dance! Celebrate! It is I! Be not afraid—at least, be not afraid. If you cannot dance, if you cannot celebrate, if you cannot sing a song, welcoming, then at least, be not afraid; be of good cheer." This has to be understood.

When the disciple is in the darkest hour of the night he becomes capable of attracting the energy of the master towards him. He has earned it, but he can receive it only if he is of good cheer. If he has hard work behind him and he has been working with his total energy, total involvement and commitment, he has earned that the master should come to him. That is necessary but not enough. If he becomes afraid, he will again miss. If he becomes afraid when the master is there, he is in need, but because of the fear the contact is impossible. Be of good cheer. Energy can be received only when you are in a happy mood, welcoming, ready to receive: like a bride waiting for the bridegroom, like a beloved for the lover—all . . . the whole waiting, as if the total energy has become just an awaiting. Be of good cheer, because without that the master cannot be of much help. He will be standing there with his hand ready to catch hold of you, but if you are not of good cheer your hand is not available.

So, two things: first, the disciple has to work totally, not withholding anything; the commitment must be absolute. You should move in it without any fear of consequences and without any expectations of the results. You should take a jump, you should dare. A master is a challenge and a disciple is an adventure. A master is a call, and a disciple is one who dares to go into the dark. He has heard the call—he's not very certain of the direction because it is all dark—but he has heard the call. He starts groping and moving. When you have done all that you can do and beyond which nothing is possible, immediately the help of the master becomes available. But then too you can miss. Many times you had earned it and missed it, because unless you are of good cheer the energy will return back. Be a host, be of good cheer. The guest has come to the door; receive him with love and gratitude.

> *And Peter answered him and said,*
> *Lord, if it be thou,*
> *bid me come unto thee on the water.*

Only one disciple out of the twelve, only one—and that too not absolutely certain. This Peter became the very rock of the Christian Church. He hesitated, doubted, demanded a proof, but at least he did that much. The other eleven remained trembling and in fear. The word 'peter' means: the rock. His name was Simon. Jesus called him Peter, the rock. And Jesus told his disciples, "I will call him Peter because he is going to become the rock of the great family I am going to create, the very foundation of the church."

> *And Peter answered him and said, Lord,*
> *if it be thou . . .*

'If' is there. Even in the greatest of disciples, the 'if' remains. "If it be thou"—he needs some proof. This is one of the most unfortunate things, but it is so: that even when you have had enough of proofs, the mind is not satisfied. It goes on asking again and again and again. They had seen many miracles happening around Jesus, they had heard him, they had looked into him, they had been recipients of his love, they had followed him into the unknown parts of God. But still Peter says, "If it be thou, bid me come unto thee on the water. So let it be a proof, so if you are really you, then do this miracle: bid me come unto thee on the water. If I can also walk on the water, then only will I believe that it is you."

And he said, Come.

... a very simple word, unconditional, with no 'if' and no 'but'. That is how Jesus is. He simply said, "Come." Just look at the simplicity of the word, with nothing behind, nothing before.

And he said, Come.
And when Peter was come down
out of the ship,
he walked on the water,
to go to Jesus.

If you listen to the master you can walk on the water. The world is the sea. If you listen to the master, the key can be delivered to you. And the key is as simple as the word 'come'; there are no conditions attached to it. Jesus has not said anything, he simply says, "Come." And Peter walked, walked on water.

But when he saw the wind boisterous,
he was afraid ...

Even walking on the water, himself walking now, and still the doubt. I face such problems every day. People come to me and say, "Everything has become beautifully silent: meditation is growing, the anger has disappeared, the sex has become a faraway thing, as if it never belonged to me. But is it all true, or am I simply imagining?" They come to me and they say, "We talk to our friends and they say 'Beware. This man has hypnotised you'." It is their experience that they have become silent, that the anger has disappeared, that the sex has become less and less a boss, more and more a servant, and it is up to them—they can fire the servant any day, and there is not even a union to protest and fight against them! But they become suspicious—

a doubt arises: "Am I imagining? Am I hypnotised? Am I dreaming all this?" They cannot believe even when the experiences are happening to them. How can they believe that it has happened to somebody else? Peter walked but could not believe himself. He must have thought, "Maybe it is just a dream, or maybe this fellow is playing a trick."

> *But when he saw the wind boisterous,*
> *he was afraid;*
> *and beginning to sink, he cried, saying,*
> *Lord, save me.*

And the moment he became afraid, he started sinking . . . because it is faith, it is trust, that saves. Once the fear enters, you start sinking. It depends on you. If you have trust you can walk over all the seas of the world—sinking is impossible. Even the water is not going to touch your feet; your feet will become a lotus. But if you become afraid, immediately—not even a single moment's time will be lost—you will be sinking. Doubt is sinking. Faith saves, doubt drowns.

> *But when he saw the wind boisterous,*
> *he was afraid;*
> *and beginning to sink, he cried, saying,*
> *Lord, save me.*

> *And immediately*
> *Jesus stretched forth his hand,*
> *and caught him,*
> *and said unto him,*
> *O thou of little faith,*
> *wherefore didst thou doubt?*

From where did this doubt come, and why? You were walking yourself and even then you couldn't trust? *O thou of little faith*—your faith is very little, but even that little faith can create such a miracle. Peter walked, not even very far, a few steps. But to walk a few steps on water is enough—if you can walk one step, you can walk all over the ocean. O man of little faith . . . faith was very little but still the miracle happened. Even a small seed of faith, and you can become a great tree of divine experience, of the flowering of the ultimate. And if with little faith this is possible, then what to say about great faith, of total faith? Then if total faith exists, immediately that seed will become the tree; there will be no time gap. The time gap exists because of little faith, the time gap exists because you cannot believe it right now. If you could believe it right now, the world disappears and only God is. The ocean disappears. You are on plain ground, because the world is not more than a dream. With doubt, the dream continues; with trust, suddenly you are awake.

I have heard one anecdote: A man went to a great physician because he was suffering from much melancholy, sadness, depression, despair. The physician examined him; there was nothing wrong. The physician said, "I don't see anything wrong in your system, and I am not going to suggest any drugs for you. Rather, there is a show going on in the town and there is a man, Grimaldi. He is a comedian. You go, and just allow that comedian to help you laugh. If you can laugh, your melancholy will disappear, your depression will disappear, and that is going to help you more than any drugs because there is nothing wrong in your system. There is just one thing that you have forgotten: how to laugh. You have simply forgotten the language of laughter, that's all. You have to learn it, that's all. No treatment is needed. You go to the show of Grimaldi."

The man said, "My God, I *am* Grimaldi!"

And the same is the case with you. You have just forgotten a language of how to be divine. You are gods.

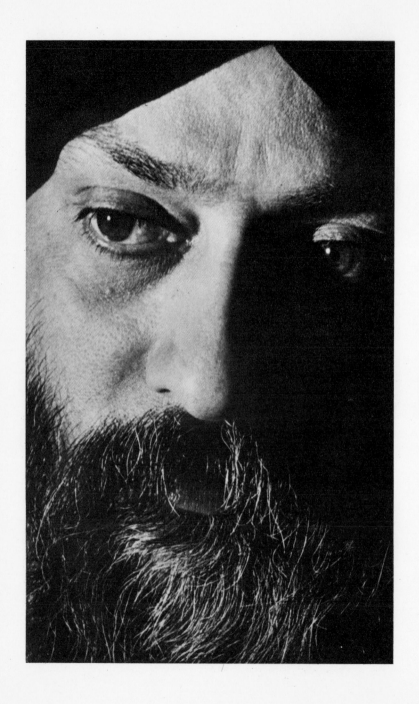

2 *Accept yourself as you are, and accept totally, unconditionally.*

Many times I feel guilty because I cannot receive you.

HE WORD 'GUILT' should never be used. The very word has wrong associations; and once you use it you are caught in it. Guilt is not a natural phenomenon: it is created by the priests. Through guilt they have exploited humanity. The whole history of pseudo-religion is contained in the word guilt: it is the most poisoned word. Beware of it; never use it, because in your unconscious mind it also has deep roots. You cannot find guilt in any animal: the animal simply is. It has no ideals, it has no arts; it exists, and simply exists. It has no perfections to be attained and hence the animal is beautiful, innocent.

Ideals corrupt. Once you have an ideal to fulfil you will never be at ease, and you will never be at home, and you can never be contented. Dissatisfaction follows ideals like a shadow, and the more dissatisfied you are with yourself, the more it becomes impossible to reach the ideal: this is the vicious circle. If you are not dissatisfied with yourself, if you accept yourself as you are, the ideal can be fulfilled immediately. And I emphasise the word 'immediately': with no time gap, right this moment, here and now, you can realize that you are perfect; it is not something to be attained in the future, it is something that you have always been carrying within you. Perfection is your nature—perfect you are.

That is the difference between a pseudo-religion and an authentic religion. The pseudo-religion says you have to be perfect, and creates guilt because you are not perfect. It creates morality because you are not perfect, and creates a deep anguish, a continuous trembling and fear because you are not perfect; and it creates hell and heaven. If you become perfect you will be awarded by heaven; if you don't become perfect you are to be punished in hell.

Authentic religion says you are perfect, not that you have to be. You cannot be imperfect, because out of God imperfection is impossible. If God has created the world, how can it be imperfect? And if you come from God, how can you be imperfect? You are gods—that art thou, *tattvamasi*. And this is a realization, an understanding, not an achievement; it is not something to be worked out. If you are silent, this very moment it is realized: you are perfect. And once you realize it, that you are perfect, you live perfectly, because whatsoever you do comes from you, arises from you.

So please, never use the word guilt: that word is dangerous, that word has been misleading you for centuries. If you cannot receive me, if you cannot understand me, let it be so; it is perfect. It may not be needed, it may not be your need. You are thirsty; then you seek water. Maybe the water is seeking you, and you are not thirsty. So what is wrong in it?

This has to be remembered: if you cannot receive me, then that's how it has to be. Then you are not at the stage where you need me. Don't create any guilt. When you need me, you will receive me, otherwise it is not possible. Every state is right;

every stage is right—wherever you are is right; and whatsoever you need, you are capable of receiving it. When your needs grow, your receptivity will grow. Don't jump ahead; don't try to overtake yourself. Then you will be in a very stupid state of mind, and then you will create your own anguish, and you will feel guilty. There is nothing in the world for which one needs to feel guilty.

Accept yourself as you are, and accept totally, unconditionally. That is the way God wants you to be: the way you are, exactly, precisely. That's how you are needed here in this moment. Don't try to change. The very effort to change is foolish, because who is going to change? You will change. The very effort is foolish, because you are trying to pull yourself up by your shoelaces. You may jump a little, but back again you will be on the same earth—and in a worse condition, because guilt will come in— you couldn't succeed, you failed.

If you are here, at least learn one thing from me—total acceptance. And total acceptance brings transformation of its own accord: that's the beauty of it. When you accept yourself you start moving—not that you force; not that you push the river; not that you fight—you flow with life. Wherever it leads is the goal. I am not giving you any goal. I am not giving you any ideal.

All perfectionists are neurotic. The very effort to become perfect is obsessive—it creates neurosis, it creates a sort of madness. Then you will never be sane. The only sanity there is, is to accept yourself as you are. Don't condemn, and don't judge. Don't make standards to judge and don't make criteria to judge. Suddenly you see that you have started moving, that the river is flowing. And the river reaches to the ocean of its own accord; nobody needs to force it. The more you try to change yourself, the more you will be in a vicious circle. And then guilt is created; and when you feel guilty, you feel condemned, and when you feel condemned, in that condemnation life becomes a hell. The hell does not exist somewhere; it exists in a wrong attitude. Then you live in hell, then your whole being is surrounded by a nightmare.

Drop that nightmare. Start living and flowing—a deep let-go, acceptance. And wherever you move, don't be worried, because God is everywhere. Wherever you reach, don't be worried: he is everywhere. You cannot miss him. How can you miss him? That is impossible. You can go on forgetting him, but you cannot miss him—he is in you, he is everywhere; only he is. But when you create the idea of guilt, for whatsoever reason, then you create a gap; then you are surrounded by your own darkness. Drop that word guilt, and always remember that words are very potential and powerful.

Just the other day I was reading about Rembrandt. He had become old, and he was working on one of his most famous paintings: The Anatomy Lesson. He was very tired the day it was completed, and he looked very exhausted. His disciple said, "Master, you look very exhausted, tired." Rembrandt, as if suddenly becoming alive, said, "Exhausted? No, never. Spent, yes. But exhausted, no." The disciple could not understand the difference. He said, "The dictionary says they both mean the same." Rembrandt said, "Forget about the dictionary, I say it through my experience: exhausted means wasted, empty, unfulfilled. Spent means flowered, completed, fulfilled." And what a difference!

Don't say you feel guilty; never use a wrong word. Drop guilt, and with the guilt you drop Christianity; with the guilt you drop Hinduism; with the guilt you drop Jainism; with the guilt you drop all nonsense that has been gathering around you. Immediately you become religious—not a Christian, not a Hindu, not a Mohammedan. Drop guilt and you become religious. Carry guilt, then guilt has many shapes—it is sold in the market in many forms and with many labels: Hindu, Christian, Mohammedan, Jain, Buddhist. No guilt . . . and suddenly you accept existence, and existence accepts you. A deep covenant, a deep trust arises between you and the whole. If I am teaching anything here, if it can be called a teaching at all, a very simple teaching it is: to be yourself, and never try to become anything else. If you cannot understand me it's okay, you don't need. Whenever you need, it happens. If you can understand something which you don't need now, it will be dangerous. Let everything happen when it is needed; let everything follow its natural course.

J am saying so many things, and I am saying them to so many people—you are not all at the same stage. Somebody is young, somebody is old; the young have not seen the life, the frustration of it—the old have seen the frustration of it. When I say life is anguish, the old will understand, but the young will feel, somehow, that they can't receive it. But that's natural—how can you receive it? A child may be here, and I may be saying something tremendously serious, and the child cannot understand it— rather, he would like to play and jump around. But that's how it should be; nothing is wrong in it. Wherever you are, there is no other way to be anywhere else; you can only be there. Be there. If you try to be somewhere else, you cannot be somewhere else. On the contrary, you will miss that which you could have been. So be, wherever you are; whatsoever you can understand, understand, and whatsoever you can receive, receive, and move, and flow. Sometimes it will happen that you will hear me today, and you will understand me years afterwards. It will remain like a seed if you have heard it—it will wait for its right time, for its right season: it will wait for ripening. Don't be worried about it. And if you start feeling guilt, then you are creating such turmoil that even the seed may be lost.

I am not a priest. I don't want you to feel guilty, because the priest exists on your guilt. The more you feel guilty, the more the priest becomes powerful, because then he has the keys to help you, to bring you out of your guilt. First he creates guilt, then he gives you the keys to come out of it. First he creates the disease, then he sells the medicine.

I am cutting the root of the disease itself. I am not here to sell any medicine to you, but just to tell you how to cut the very root of the disease. So remember, each stage is right, each stage is necessary. Pass through each, and don't try to jump ahead.

Can trust be cultivated?

A cultivated trust will not be trust; it will be false, it will be insincere. It will just be on the surface; it will never touch your centre. Whatsoever is cultivated remains superficial, because whatsoever is cultivated remains of the mind. Trust cannot be cultivated, just as love cannot be cultivated: you can't teach people how to love. Dangerous will be the days when people are taught how to love, because they will learn the lesson, they will repeat it accurately—it will be technological but it will not be of the heart.

Anything that belongs to the depth has to come out of its own accord. So what is to be done? I understand the question you are asking. Then what to do? The only thing that can be done is to remove hindrances. Trust cannot be brought out; hindrances can be removed. When there is no hindrance, it comes, it flows. Trust cannot be cultivated; doubts can be dropped.

So one has to understand the doubting mind, the very mechanism of doubt, why you doubt. One has to see through and through why one doubts, because doubt is the hindrance. When doubt disappears, suddenly trust is there. It has always been there.

Only a rock was hindering the path, and the fountain could not flow. You come with trust. Every child is born with trust, every child is trusting, so trust need not be cultivated. That's how everybody is born: it is in-built. You are trust.

But by and by, the child learns how to doubt. We teach, in fact—the society, the family, the school, the university, they all teach how to doubt. Because unless you doubt, you cannot be very clever and cunning; unless you doubt, you cannot be left in this great world of competition: you will be destroyed. So doubt has to be learned; and once you learn it, by and by, trust is forgotten. It remains deep within you, but you cannot reach to it—too many obstacles. You cannot cultivate it; it cannot be taught. The only thing is, you have to reverse the process—you have learned doubt, now unlearn it.

Trust was there, trust is there, trust will be there. All that has to be done is to be done with doubt; nothing is to be done with trust. Why do you doubt? Why are you so afraid?—because doubt means fear. Whenever you love somebody, you don't doubt, because fear disappears. Whenever there is love, fear is not. But when you don't love, you doubt; when you don't know a person, you doubt more—a stranger, then you doubt even more; unfamiliar, unknown, then you doubt more. Whenever there is fear, there is doubt. Deep down, doubt is fear. If you go still deeper, doubt is death, because you are afraid of death. And it seems that everybody is trying to kill you; fighting —everybody competitive—everybody trying to push you aside, dethrone you. Doubt is death.

The whole mechanism has to be understood. Then what to do? Why is one afraid of death? You have never known death. You may have seen somebody else dying, but you have never seen death. When somebody is dying, do you really know that he is dying—or simply disappearing into some other world? Doubt is without base; fear is without base—it is just an assumption of the mind. When somebody dies, do you think he is dying, or simply disappearing into another world, moving to another plane of life, or to another body? You will have to know it in deep meditation. When thinking stops, suddenly you see that you are separate from the body.

So I don't say trust first; I say meditate first. That is the difference between meditation and prayer. People who teach prayer, they say, "Trust first, otherwise how can you pray?" Trust is needed as a basic condition, otherwise how can you pray? If you don't trust God, how can you pray? I teach meditation, because meditation doesn't require trust as a basic necessity. Meditation is a science, not a superstition. Meditation says you experiment with your mind—it is too full of thoughts; thoughts can be dispersed, the clouds can be dispersed, and you can attain to an empty sky of your inner being. And it needs no trust—just a little courage, a little effort, a little daring, a little persistence and perseverance, a little patience, yes, but no trust. You don't believe in God? That is not a hindrance to meditation. You don't believe in soul? That is not a hindrance in meditation. You don't believe at all? That is not an obstacle. You can meditate, because meditation simply says how to go withinwards: whether there is a soul or not doesn't matter; whether there is a God or not doesn't matter.

One thing is certain: that you are. Whether you will be after death, or not, does not matter. Only one thing matters: right this moment, you are. Who are you? To enter into it is meditation: to go deeper into your own being. Maybe it is just momentary; maybe you are not eternal; maybe death finishes everything: we don't make any condition that you have to believe. We say only that you have to experiment. Just try. One day it happens: thoughts are not there, and suddenly when thoughts disappear, the body and you are separate, because thoughts are the bridge. Through thoughts you are joined with the body; it is the link. Suddenly the link disappears—you are there, the body is there, and there is an infinite abyss between the two. Then you know that the body will die, but you cannot die.

Then it is not something like a dogma; it is not a creed, it is an experience—self-evident. On that day, death disappears; on that day, doubt disappears, because now you are not always to be defending yourself. Nobody can destroy you; you are indestructible. Then trust arises, overflows. And to be in trust is to be in ecstasy; to be in trust is to be in God; to be in trust is to be fulfilled.

So I don't say cultivate trust. I say experiment with meditation. From another angle try to understand it. Doubt means thinking. The more you doubt, the more you can think. All great thinkers are sceptical—have to be. Scepticism creates thinking. When you say no, then thinking arises; if you say yes, finished—there is no need to think. When you say no, then you have to think. Thinking is negative. Doubt is a basic necessity for thinking. People who cannot doubt, cannot think; they cannot become great thinkers. So, more doubt means more thinking, more thinking means more doubt. Meditation is a way to come out of thinking. Once the clouds of thoughts are not there, and the process of thinking ceases, even for a single moment, you have a glimpse of your being.

One of the greatest thinkers in the West, Descartes, has said, "I think, therefore I am." *Cogito ergo sum.* And Descartes is the father of modern Western philosophy. 'I think, therefore I am.' Just the opposite has been the experience in the East. Buddha, Nagarjuna, Sankara, Lao Tzu, Chuang Tzu, they will laugh, they will laugh tremendously when they hear Descartes' dictum, 'I think, therefore I am'; because they say, "I don't think, therefore I am."

Because when thinking ceases, only then does one know who one is. In a non-thinking state of consciousness one realizes one's being, not by thinking, but by non-thinking. Meditation is non-thinking; it is an effort to create a state of no-mind. Doubt is mind. In fact, to say 'doubting mind' is wrong; it is repetitive—

mind is doubt; doubt is mind. When doubt ceases, mind ceases; or when mind ceases, doubt ceases. And then self-evident truth arises within, a pinnacle of light, eternity, timelessness; and then there is trust.

Right now how can you trust? Right now you don't know who you are—how can you trust? And you ask, "Can trust be cultivated?" Never. Never try to cultivate it. Many have done that foolishness. Then they become false, inauthentic, pseudo. It is better to be a no-sayer, but sincere, because there is at least a possibility, through sincerity, that some day you may become an authentic yea-sayer. But never say yes until it arises from within and overwhelms you.

The whole world is full of pseudo-religious people: churches, temples, *gurudwaras*, mosques, full of religious people. And can't you see the world is absolutely irreligious? With so many religious people, and the world is so irreligious, how is this miracle happening? Everybody is religious, and the total is irreligiousness. The religion is false. People have cultivated trust. Trust has become a belief, not an experience. They have been taught to believe; they have not been taught to know—that's where humanity has missed. Never believe. If you cannot trust, it is better to doubt, because through doubt, some day or other, the possibility will arise; because you cannot live with doubt eternally. Doubt is disease; it is an illness. In doubt you can never feel fulfilled; in doubt you will always tremble, in doubt you will always remain in anguish and divided and indecisive. In doubt you will remain in a nightmare; so one day or other you will start seeking how to go beyond it. So I say it is good to be an atheist rather than a theist, a pseudo-theist.

You have been taught to believe—from the very childhood, everybody's mind has been conditioned to believe: believe in God, believe in soul, believe in this and believe in that. Now that belief has entered into your bones and your blood, but it remains a belief: you have not known. And unless you know, you cannot be liberated. Knowledge liberates; only knowing liberates. All beliefs are borrowed; others have given them to you. They are not your flowerings. And how can a borrowed thing lead you towards the real, the absolutely real? Drop all that you have taken from others. It is better to be a beggar than to be rich; rich not by your own earning, but rich through stolen goods, rich through borrowed things, rich through tradition, rich through heritage. No, it is better to be a beggar, but to be on one's own. That poverty has a richness in it because it is true, and your richness of belief is very poor. Those beliefs can never go very deep; they remain skin-deep at the most. Scratch a little, and the disbelief comes out.

You believe in God. Then your business fails, and suddenly, the disbelief is there. You say, "I don't believe, I cannot believe in God." You believe in God, and your beloved dies, and the disbelief comes up. You believe in God, and just by the death of your beloved the belief is destroyed? It is not worth much. Trust can never be destroyed—once it is there, nothing can destroy it; nothing, absolutely nothing can destroy it.

So remember, there is a great difference between trust and belief. Trust is personal; belief is social. Trust you have to grow in; belief you can remain in, whatsoever you are, and belief can be imposed on you. Drop beliefs. The fear will be there; because if you drop belief, doubt arises. Each belief is forcing doubt somewhere, repressing doubt. Don't be worried about it; let the doubt come. Everybody has to pass through a dark night before he reaches the sunrise. Everybody has to pass through doubt. Long is the journey, dark is the night. But when after the long journey and the dark night the morning arises, then you know it was all worthwhile. Trust cannot be cultivated. And never try to cultivate it—that is what has been done by the whole of humanity. Cultivated trust becomes belief. Discover it within yourself, don't cultivate it. Go deeper into your being, to the very source of your being, and discover it.

*W*hen Jawaharlal Nehru died, a small slip of paper was found on his pillow. In his own handwriting he had noted a few lines of Robert Frost:

> *The woods are lovely, dark and deep.*
> *But I have promises to keep,*
> *And miles to go before I sleep.*
> *And miles to go before I sleep.*

He must have written it just before he died. 'The woods are lovely . . .' Everybody has to go alone; you cannot keep company. Because you have to go inwards you can only go alone. 'The woods are lovely . . .' because the woods are of your inner being. If you go for an outer pilgrimage, you can have company; somebody can be with you: a beloved, a friend, a relative, a fellow-traveller. But the woods are lovely because the woods are of your inner being—you have to go alone.

'Dark and deep . . .' and there is much darkness within. You have always heard that if you go inwards, you will find infinite light. That is only half of the truth. You will find infinite light at the very centre, but before that centre is reached, much darkness has to be passed through. It is not that you just close your eyes and there is infinite light; no, there will be infinite darkness first because that is the price one has to pay. The dark night is the price one has to pay for the morning. And remember, until you pay for it, it won't be worthwhile—unless you pay for it you cannot value it. If a morning is given to you, and you have not travelled and struggled for it, you will not be able to see it.

Somewhere, Vincent van Gogh, one of the greatest Dutch painters, has written that he was in some part of France where sunsets are tremendously beautiful. One day when he was

painting . . . a woman used to help him—she asked van Gogh,
"Can I run home and show my people: my father, my mother,
my sisters and my brothers, this beautiful sunset?" Van Gogh
said, "There is no need. The sunset is there; they will see it by
themselves." The woman laughed, and she said, "I am thirty. I
have lived on this seashore for thirty years, but until you came,
we had never seen the sunset."

Just because a thing is there it is not necessary that you will
see it: one has to learn, one has to grow. One needs a van Gogh
to show you, to make you sensitive, to make you aware. I love
that story. This is how it has been happening—God is there, but
a van Gogh, a Buddha, is needed to show you. And then you
will see; you will be surprised, amazed, that this has been always
there. Why did you miss? One needs growth. When you go in,
infinite light is there. The Upanishads are true. When Jesus says,
"The kingdom of God is within," he is absolutely true. But when
you go in, first you will enter the kingdom of the devil, not of
God.

Dark night of the soul. . . .

If you pass through it, if you dare to pass through it, if you
are courageous to go alone in it, only then you will be capable,
you will have earned; then you will have a right to claim the
morning.

> *The woods are lovely, dark and deep.*
> *But I have promises to keep,*
> *And miles to go before I sleep.*

Before you can rest in your innermost core, in your innermost
shrine of being, miles to go, miles to grow, miles to flow. . . .

'But I have promises to keep . . .' To whom have you given
promises?—every seed has promised to be a tree—not to anybody: to one's own destiny, to one's own self. Every seed has
given a promise to be a tree, and to flower, and to blossom, and
to spread into millions of seeds. It is not a promise given verbally

to anybody; it is a deep existential promise given to one's own being, to one's destiny. Call it God, or call it whatsoever you like, but everybody is a traveller on a great pilgrimage.

> But I have promises to keep,
> And miles to go before I sleep.
> And miles to go before I sleep.

There is a dark night to be crossed, to be gone through. Only then will you be able, will your eyes be capable, to see light.

Remember, don't deceive yourself by beliefs. Beliefs can be given to you free; you need not earn them. Trust is a growth, a ripening of your being. It is painful, remember. Beliefs are very convenient—to become a Mohammedan, to become a Christian, to become a Hindu—nothing is needed, just the accident of birth is enough. That you are born into a family and you become a Hindu or a Mohammedan, is just an accident. If a child is born into a Hindu family and brought up by a Mohammedan family, he will become a Mohammedan. He will never know he was ever a Hindu—just an accident.

No, life cannot be that cheap. Trust cannot be that cheap. Love cannot be that cheap; one has to stake one's whole soul for it. Never try to cultivate trust; never try to make trust function, because that will be belief. Drop doubt. Enter into doubt; realize the futility of doubt; realize the futility of thinking and try to come to a state of no-mind; and then trust arises. You simply remove the hindrances. Nothing positive is needed to be done, only something negative: something has to be removed. When the passage is clear, trust flows. You melt and you start flowing.

It happened that when Alexander came to India he met a sann-yasin, a great sage. The sage's name was Dandamis; that is how Greek historians have pronounced it. Alexander asked him,

"Do you believe in God?" The sage remained silent. Alexander said, "I cannot see, so how can I believe? How do you believe without seeing him?" The naked sage laughed. He took Alexander by his hand towards the marketplace. Alexander followed —maybe he was taking him somewhere where he could show him God. A small boy was flying a kite, and the kite had gone so far away that it was impossible to see it. The sage stopped there, and asked that boy, "Where is the kite? Because we cannot see it, and without seeing how can we believe? Where is the kite? How do you still believe that the kite exists?" The boy said, "I can feel the pull of it." And the sage said to Alexander, "I can also feel the pull of it."

Trust is nothing but the feel of the pull. You don't see—one has never seen God; only the pull is felt. But that is enough, that is more than enough. But then you have to be in a certain state where the pull can be felt. It cannot be learned from scriptures; it is not a doctrine. Nobody can explain it: you have to feel the pull.

The old sage laughed. Alexander also realized that it had been a revelation. But the sage said, "Wait; no need to believe in me. You take the thread in your hand and feel the pull, because who knows? This boy may be deceiving. Never believe. Feel the pull." If Alexander had gone away just listening to the boy, it would have been a belief. But he felt the pull: the kite was there on the other end, the pull was here on this end. He could feel the force. He thanked the old sage.

Meditation is a state where you allow yourself to feel the pull of existence. That pull has been called by many names. In the Upanishads they say: *ekam sad viparah bahudha vadanti*: that one is one. But sages have called it many names.

···✳···

Bhagwan, I seem to have found my question: the
closer I seem to get to my beloved, the closer I seem to
get to myself—and the further and further away I seem
to get from you. Yet according to you, the closer one
gets to oneself, the closer one gets to you. So something,
somewhere, is not what it seems. What is it?

Let me share one anecdote with you. Henry David Thoreau
was dying—on his deathbed. An old friend asked him, "Thoreau,
do you believe in the other world, the hereafter?" Thoreau was
just going to die, almost on the verge. He opened his eyes and
said, "One world at a time brother, one world at a time."

If love is happening, forget all about me. One world at a
time sister, one world at a time.

Sooner or later, what you are understanding as love now, will
disappear. But don't believe what I am saying—go through it. It
always disappears; it is just like the dewdrops in the morning. They
look so beautiful, and while they last they are—pearls. But as
the sun rises, they evaporate and disappear without even a trace
behind. Love is beautiful while it lasts. I am not against love; I
am all for it. But it is like dewdrops. What can I do? I am helpless.

So while it lasts, enjoy it. At your stage of mind it must be
a need: it will fulfil something. Never drop out of it unless you
have ripened, unless it disappears of its own accord; and then,
don't complain; and then, don't feel frustrated. When love, love
that you call love disappears, then a different kind of love arises.
Only that love can bring you near me.

Right now, the love that you feel can be of two types.
Either it can be just a biological attraction of two bodies, feminine
and male, yin and yang, positive and negative; of two energies—
because they are opposite they attract each other. That is the
lowest type of love. Nothing wrong in it, remember, because the
lowest love is also very beautiful. And there are people who are
lower than the lowest love; there are people, millions of them,

who have not even known the lowest love. That is the lowest rung of the ladder.

There are people who are after money; they have not known even the biological attraction. There are people who are after power, politics, and have not known even the biological attraction. It is the lowest rung, but it is still a rung of a ladder which is of love; so, good. It has been called sex; the word has become very degraded, because religions have condemned it too much. I have no condemnation for anything. I am all for using everything, and going beyond. Step over everything and go beyond: every obstacle can become a stepping-stone. Use it.

So either it can be the physical, the biological attraction of the body—then it is sexual. Good, but much more is possible; don't cling there. Remember:

> *. . . promises to keep,*
> *miles to go before you sleep.*

Then there is a second rung of the ladder: the attraction of two minds. That is what is called love; the attraction of two minds, the feminine and the male. As bodies are feminine and male, minds are also feminine and male. The male mind is aggressive; the feminine mind is receptive and passive—they fit together. It is higher than the first. The first is almost of the animal kingdom; the second is human. In the first, there can be an oblivion, a forgetfulness, a deep intoxication for a few seconds. In the second, there is much more of poetry, much more of romance, much more of aesthetic sensitivity. Very few people reach to the second—where the beloved becomes the friend; where the lover becomes the friend. In the first, possessiveness and jealousy spoil the whole game. Possessiveness has to disappear otherwise the second will not be possible. Then you are two fellow-travellers. In the first you face each other; in the second, you both face something else.

For example, if two persons who are attracted to each other's body are sitting in a full-moon night, they will be looking at each other, holding hands, looking at each other. In the second stage, they may be holding hands, or they may not be holding hands, but they will not be looking at each other; they will both be looking at the moon—a tremendous difference. Now they are being held together by something else higher than both, deeper than both. This second type of love is very beautiful, but still, like dewdrops, it disappears.

If you are frustrated in the first and don't become hopeless, you then enter the second. If you are frustrated in the first, get so much caught in the frustration, and become hopeless, you never enter the second. Then you remain a body; you never come to know that you are also a mind. In the second, if you are frustrated, as you will be—it has to be so, because the second is not the goal, not the end—if you are frustrated and you become hopeless, then you are caught in the second. But if you are frustrated and don't become hopeless, and your search and enquiry goes higher and higher, and you try to see why this love failed . . . the first love failed because it was only bodily—it could not satisfy the mind; the second failed because it was only of the mind—it could not satisfy the soul: and when the third type of love arises, then you will be near me.

When I am with you I am speechless. I feel my mouth and throat become inappropriate and almost lose their function. Yet language is my best implement, also my best weapon, and without it I feel crippled. Am I as foolish as I feel to be, squandering these chances of talking to you?

No. To be with me, you have to be in silence. If you talk,

you miss the chance, because words become barriers. Words are not means of communication, they are means of avoiding communication. Whenever you want to be with someone, you want to be silent: only in silence there is communion. Only in deep silence there is a merger and a meeting and the boundaries dissolve. Something of me enters you, and something of you enters me.

If you come to me and talk, and talk, and talk, you don't allow me to enter. And you don't allow yourself to be vulnerable. But it is natural when you come to see me for the first time and suddenly you feel that you cannot talk, that you cannot communicate through words. You feel as if you are not communicating at all, because all your life you have been communicating through words and you don't know that there is another dimension of communion, there is another way. With me words are useless.

To be with me, the only way is to be in deep silence, deep receptivity, in a deep opening so that I can pour myself into you. If you are too full of words and talking too many things, you will miss me. Silence is the language with me.

So don't be worried about it. It is exactly as it should be. Whenever people come to me, there are two types. The foolish ones are those who talk too much; the wiser ones are those who keep quiet, who remain silent. But you cannot deceive me just by being quiet because inside you go on chattering. It won't help. The question is not whether you utter, or not; the question is whether there are words, or not.

Learn more and more to be in a state of non-chattering—the inner talk has to stop. Then your mind is not hindering; then you are available; then your deepest shrine of being is available to me. But by and by, you will learn. In the beginning, it happens so. You have always been talking, and if you are very articulate in talking, then of course you feel crippled. If you are very articulate and you can talk beautifully, artistically, if you

can play perfectly with language and then suddenly you come
to me and your throat does not allow you to speak . . . and something goes wrong and the mechanism doesn't function: you feel
that you are crippled. But you are not crippled—the impact of
my presence has simply given a shock to the mechanism of your
mind. And it is good. Don't try to bring it back. Let it go. Be
quiet, still, silent and waiting. Be feminine.

A disciple needs to know how to be feminine, that is, how
to be like a womb so that he can receive and he can become pregnant. Unless you become pregnant, nothing will happen to you.
You can learn so many things here with me, but that learning
will be more and more a burden to you, not a freedom; it will
create more chains for you. Then you may not be chained by
Christianity; you will be chained by my words. Then you may
not believe in the Vedas, but then my words will become the
Vedas.

No, I am here to make you utterly liberated, including from
myself.

You are my disciple only if you remember this: that one day
or other you have to become liberated from me also. Only then
have you obeyed me; only then will I be happy with you. But
if you cling to my words. . . . What I say is not very meaningful,
what I say is not significant: what I am not saying, what I cannot say—nobody can say—only that is significant. Listen to that
which is not said. Listen to the gaps in the intervals. Read between
the words and between the lines. If you forget the words, nothing
is lost; but if you forget that which is between the words, much
is lost.

Your gestalt has to change. That is the difference between a
student and a disciple: a change of gestalt, a change of attention,
of focusing, a shift. The student listens to the word; the disciple
listens to the gap between two words. The student reads the
lines; the disciple, between the lines. If to a student I give an
empty book, he will not be able to understand it. But if to a

disciple I give an empty book, *The Nothing Book*, he will preserve it as a treasure.

In the Sufi tradition there is a book called *The Book of the Books*. Nothing is written in it; empty pages, almost three hundred empty pages. You go on reading, but you can never finish it. It has been passed from one generation of masters to another. It has been lovingly preserved, worshipped, because it says nothing, but it shows much. It says nothing, but it indicates much. If all the Vedas and the Bibles and the Gitas and the Korans disappear, nothing will be lost. But if this *Book of the Books* is lost, everything is lost. Because if you can read this book of nothing, *The Book of the Books*, Vedas can be rediscovered, Bibles can be written again; because all the blueprints are there. Out of the empty mind the Gita can be produced again, because that is how it was produced in the first place. A man, Krishna, became empty, and answered Arjuna's questions from his emptiness—responded. Out of that emptiness, out of that *Book of the Books*, the book Gita was born.

That's how it happened in Mohammed's life. He was sitting on a mountain, meditating, fasting; absolutely empty. Suddenly he heard deep somewhere within himself—which was also beyond himself. . . . From his own soul, but as if from some beyond, came an order: "Write." But he said, "My God, but I don't know how to write. I am illiterate." And the voice said, "That's why you have been chosen. Write!"—because those who are literate are corrupted, those who know are corrupted; those who are innocent, in their ignorance, only they can hear the voice of the beyond.

*P*lease, don't get caught with my words. Always remember that what I am trying to convey is always in the gaps. Don't be caught by the banks that the river is flowing between. And *that* you can hear only when you are silent; that you can hear only when the inner talk has stopped, when your mind is not clouded.

You appeared to me yesterday to be literally as well as figuratively drunk. Were you?

I have always been—and not figuratively, not symbolically. I am a drunkard, literally, absolutely, actually; because religion is the ultimate drug. Once you have tasted of it, you are gone for ever and ever. It is the ultimate high—you never come down again. With other drugs you reach a high, but again you are thrown back. With religion, once you reach the high you never come back: it is a point of no return.

I am drunk. Look into my eyes; come close to me and smell my breath. But beware, because such people are dangerous— even their breath can make you drunk.

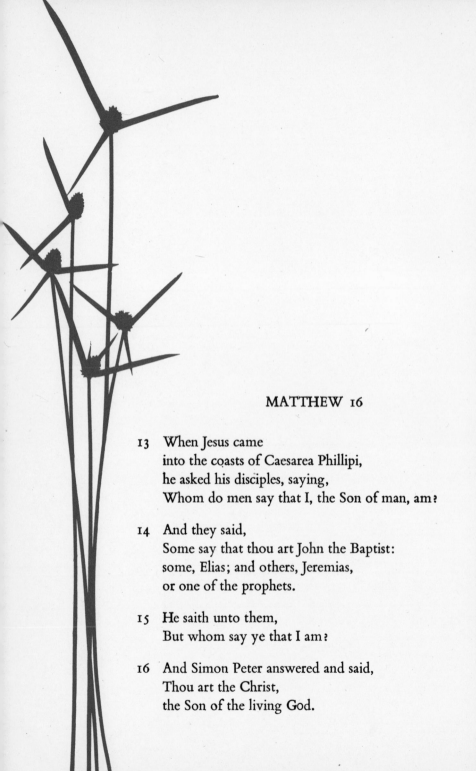

MATTHEW 16

13 When Jesus came
   into the coasts of Caesarea Phillipi,
   he asked his disciples, saying,
   Whom do men say that I, the Son of man, am?

14 And they said,
   Some say that thou art John the Baptist:
   some, Elias; and others, Jeremias,
   or one of the prophets.

15 He saith unto them,
   But whom say ye that I am?

16 And Simon Peter answered and said,
   Thou art the Christ,
   the Son of the living God.

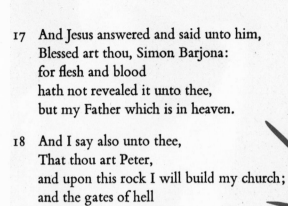

17   And Jesus answered and said unto him,
Blessed art thou, Simon Barjona:
for flesh and blood
hath not revealed it unto thee,
but my Father which is in heaven.

18   And I say also unto thee,
That thou art Peter,
and upon this rock I will build my church;
and the gates of hell
shall not prevail against it.

19   And I will give unto thee
the keys of the kingdom of heaven:
and whatsoever thou shalt bind on earth
shall be bound in heaven:
and whatsoever thou shalt loose on earth
shall be loosed in heaven.

20   Then charged he his disciples
that they should tell no man
that he was Jesus the Christ.

3   *There is no future God; there is no past God; there is only God as life herenow.*

ONCE IT HAPPENED: Aesop, the greatest master of story-telling, was going out of Athens. He met a man who was coming from Argos. They talked. The man from Argos asked Aesop, "You are coming from Athens. Please tell me something about the people there: what manner of men they are, what they are like."

Aesop asked the man, "First you tell me what type of people are there in Argos."

The man said, "Very disgusting, nauseating, violent, quarrelsome." And all these qualities flashed on the face of the man.

Aesop said, "I am sorry. You will find the people of Athens just the same."

Later on, he met another man who was also from Argos, and he also asked the same question: "You are coming from Athens and you have lived your whole life there—what manner of men are they there? What are they like?"

And Aesop again asked, "First tell me what manner of men are there in Argos."

And the man became aflame with nostalgia . . . a very loving
memory of the people of Argos. His face shone and he said,
"Very pleasant, friendly, kind, and good neighbours."

Aesop said, "I am happy to tell you that you will find the
people of Athens just the same."

The story is tremendously beautiful. It tells a very basic
truth about man: wherever you go, you will always find yourself; wherever you look, you will always encounter yourself.
The whole world is nothing but a mirror, and all relationships
are mirrors. Again and again you encounter yourself—and again
and again you misunderstand. You never realize the point, that
it is your own face that you have looked at, that it is your own
mood that you have come across.

Why have I started with this story of Aesop?—for a very
basic reason. You can recognize Jesus only if you have recognized
something of the beyond within yourself; otherwise not. You
can recognize Buddha only if a part of you has become like
Buddha; otherwise you cannot recognize. You cannot recognize
that which has not happened to you.

If you are dark, only darkness can be recognized. If you are
light, then you become capable of recognizing light. Your eyes
can see light because they are part of the sun, because something
within you has become of the nature of light. A deep transformation has happened within you. Only then is it possible to recognize a Jesus, a Buddha, a Krishna, a Mohammed. Otherwise
you will misunderstand them; you will think that you have
understood them. It will be nothing but your own reflection,
it will be nothing but your own echoes. It is your own voice that
you have heard coming from them; it is your own face that you
have looked at in their mirror.

So before you can understand Jesus, you have to understand
yourself. Before you can have the vision that Jesus has something,
at least something of the same vision has to be allowed within
you.

These sutras are very significant.

*When Jesus came
into the coasts of Caesarea Phillipi,
he asked his disciples, saying,
Whom do men say that I, the Son of man, am?*

Why did he ask this? The people were saying all sorts of things about him. People have always been gossiping. They feed on rumours and they go on expressing their opinions without knowing what they are doing.

Have you watched the same tendency in yourself? If you watch and observe, it will drop, and it is one of the basic requirements. If ever you want to know truth, you have to drop all gossiping. If you want to know what truth is, you have to stop making opinions without knowing anything. It is such a foolish attitude. You don't know anything about yourself, but if you come across a Jesus, you immediately create an opinion about him. Have you ever thought about it—about what you are doing? You go on judging, not knowing anything even about yourself, which is the nearest point of consciousness to you. Who is more close to you than yourself?—and you have not known even that.

Jesus is far away from you. Stop rumouring, because those rumours will cloud your eyes; those rumours, those opinions, will destroy your perception, your clarity.

Why does Jesus ask what people are saying about him? Whenever a man like Jesus happens, the whole world is agog with rumours. People go on talking about him. Sometimes I have come across people. . . .

Once it happened: I was travelling and I had another passenger in my compartment—only two persons, he and I. He was reading a book, so I asked him—he was reading one of my books, but he didn't know me, and he started saying things about me—I asked him, "Are you certain?"

He said, "Absolutely certain."

"Have you seen this man you are talking about?"

He said, "Yes. Not only seen, we have been class-fellows."

Once you utter a lie, you have to utter many more lies.

I told the man, "I'm the man you are talking about."

• He laughed. He said, "You are joking." He wouldn't believe me.

Whenever a man like Jesus is there, a thousand and one rumours spread. People say all sorts of things. Why do they say them?—to show that they know.

There is a story of Gogol, the Russian master. He tells that in a small town there was a very simple man and people used to think that he was an idiot. A sage visited the town, and the idiot came to the sage and asked, "I'm in constant trouble. The whole town thinks that I am an idiot, and before I have said anything, people start laughing—before I have even said anything, so I cannot say a single word. I am so afraid. I cannot move in the society, because wherever I go people ridicule me. You are a wise man. Help me. Give me some clue as to how I can protect myself. My whole life is destroyed."

The sage said something in his ear. He said, "Do only one thing: whenever somebody says something, immediately deny it; contradict it, negate it. Whatsoever it is, don't be bothered. Somebody is saying, 'Look, how beautiful the moon is!' Immediately say, 'Who says so? Prove it!' Nobody can prove it. Somebody says that Buddha or Christ are enlightened people— immediately deny it; contradict it—'Who says so? What is enlightenment?—all nonsense, rubbish!'"

The simple man said, "But I may not be able to prove that it is rubbish."

The old sage said, "You need not worry; nobody will ask you. They will be trying to prove whatsoever they are saying."

"Never say anything positively, and you will never be in

trouble. Just negate. If somebody says, 'God exists,' say, 'No. Where is God? Prove it!' "

The man tried the trick and after seven days the whole town was simply surprised. People started saying, "We never knew that this man was so wise!"

If you want to look wise, you have to utter nonsenses. And the best way is to deny, to say no, because life is such a mystery that nothing can be proved. If somebody says, "Look, this woman is so beautiful," say, "Who says so? What is there about her? Why do you call her beautiful? I don't see anything." Nobody can prove it. All the poets of the world can stand against you, but you are going to win. Things are so mysterious—they cannot be proved; they cannot be reduced to an argument.

Nobody wants to feel that he does not know. If you say that yes, Jesus is enlightened, it will be difficult to prove, almost impossible. Twenty centuries of constant argument have not proved anything. Jesus remains as mysterious, as riddlesome as he was. Twenty centuries of theology, constant argument, elaboration, explanation, analysis, interpretation—nothing has been proved. Jesus remains as mysterious as he ever was—maybe even more so—because he is lost in these explanations.

You cannot prove that Jesus is enlightened, because enlightenment is something beyond the mind. You have to taste it; you cannot talk about it; and when you taste it you become silent. But if you want to say that he is nothing, nobody, you can prove it. That is simply very easy.

So people were saying many things, contradicting, negating, arguing that this man is nothing.

When Jesus came
into the coasts of Caesarea Phillipi,
he asked his disciples, saying,
Whom do men say that I, the Son of man, am?
What are people saying about me?

And they said,
Some say that thou art John the Baptist;
some, Elias; and others, Jeremias,
or one of the prophets.

This happens always. People have only one criterion and that
is of the past. And a man like Jesus is of the present; he is not
from the past. He does not belong to any tradition—he cannot
belong. A man like Jesus is a rebellion. He cannot be part of any
tradition. But the ordinary human mind has no other criteria.
At the most, you can think about the past. You can say, "Maybe
he is John the Baptist, or Elias, or Ezekiel or Jeremias, or one of
the old, past prophets." When those prophets were present, you
never understood them. You never looked into them, directly
and immediately. You never encountered them, because to encounter them is great daring. No other courage is more dangerous than to encounter a man who has known, because he is
deathlike; he is an infinite abyss.

If you look into Jeremias or Ezekiel or Elias, you are looking
into a bottomless abyss. You will start shaking and trembling;
you will start perspiring, and you will be afraid. One step, and
you can be lost forever, and you cannot come back again.

Jesus, Buddha, and Krishna, they are absolute emptinesses.
Their ego has disappeared. They are just vast spaces of being—
no boundaries, no maps. The territory is uncharted. Look into
it and you will lose your balance. The very earth below your
feet will disappear. You will find yourself falling and falling
and falling—and the falling is endless.

So people never look directly. When Jesus is there, they talk
about John, they talk about Elias, they talk about Ezekiel, they
talk about Jeremias, they talk about Abraham, Moses—they can
talk about the whole past, but they will not look at this man
who is right now here. They have been doing the same to Moses,
to Abraham and to everybody. When Moses is there, they will

not encounter him. That is too dangerous and risky. Then they will talk of somebody else.

The disciples said,

> *Some say that thou art John the Baptist:*
> *some, Elias; and others, Jeremias,*
> *or one of the prophets.*

A few things are to be understood. Whenever a Jesus happens, he is absolutely fresh and virgin. He does not come from the past; he comes from above. That is the Hindu meaning of *avatar:* he descends. He is not part of the chain. He is not horizontal; he is vertical.

Whenever *you* become alert and aware, immediately your whole being turns. Then you are no more horizontal; suddenly you find yourself vertical. If a man is lying down and fast asleep, he is horizontal. Sleep is horizontal. It is very difficult to stand and sleep—you have to lie down. That is the most comfortable position. If you try to sleep standing up, it will be almost impossible. Sleep is horizontal, unconsciousness is horizontal. But when a man awakes, he sits, he stands up, he becomes vertical. Take it symbolically.

The same happens in the inner world. When a man is unconscious, unaware, he is horizontal; his consciousness is horizontal. When he becomes alert, aware, conscious, he stands. Then the consciousness becomes vertical.

And this is the meaning of the Christian cross: two lines, one horizontal, one vertical. The horizontal line is of unconsciousness and the vertical line is of consciousness. The horizontal line you can call 'of matter', the vertical 'of consciousness'; the horizontal line, the world, the *maya;* and the vertical, the God, the *brahma.*

The cross is very, very significant and multi-dimensional. You must have seen Jesus on the cross. Have you observed that his hands are on the horizontal line and his whole body on the vertical? Why?—because doing is horizontal and being is vertical. Hands are just representatives of doing. Whatsoever you do, you do with matter. Whatsoever you do, becomes part of the world. Whatsoever you do, moves into history. Whatsoever you do, becomes part of time; it becomes horizontal. But whatsoever you *are*—the pure being—is not part of the world. It may be in the world, but it is not of the world. It penetrates the world. That's why Hindus have given it a beautiful name—*avatar*. It comes down from above. Like a ray of light it penetrates the darkness. The ray may be in the darkness, but it is not of the darkness. It comes from above.

Zen says that by doing, you cannot attain, because whatsoever you do will move outwards. That's why Zen says even meditation is not to be done—one has to be meditative. Prayer cannot be done; one has to be prayerful. Love cannot be done; one has to be loving. The difference is between doing and being. When you are loving, it is part of the vertical. When you are meditative, it is part of the vertical. When you start meditating, it becomes horizontal.

All effort, all doing has to cease. That is the meaning of Jesus' hands on the horizontal line. And the whole, except the hands, is on the vertical. Except for what you do, all your being is part of God. Whatsoever you do is part of the world.

But only hands are seen. If I don't do anything, I will become invisible. You will not be able to see me. Not that you will not see me, but you will not recognize me. If I don't do anything, I will be as if I am not; because you know only one criterion: that something should be done.

That's why in your books of history, Buddhas are just footnotes; not more than that. That, too, seems to be a concession. Alexanders, Napoleons, they make history; Buddhas?—just footnotes. You are so kind towards them that you allow them a small space, a few lines. But they don't become the main part of history because you ask, "What have they done?" And if

Buddha is there, and Jesus is there, that too is because they have done *something*—maybe not much, but something.

There have been Buddhas who have completely disappeared —they have not even left a ripple in the history. Buddha himself talks about twenty-four Buddhas who preceded him. History does not know anything about them. They may have been absolutely silent people, people of being. Nothing is known about them, because how can you know if they don't *do* anything? *Gundas* are known—hooligans. Sages become invisible, because unless you do something, you don't leave a trace.

The more you *do*, the more the horizontal line receives you. The more you *are*, you disappear. You only see hands; you don't see anything else.

The disciples said, "People think that you are an incarnation of John the Baptist, or Elias or Jeremias. They think about you in terms of others of the past"—and that is where you miss. A man like Jesus is absolutely fresh; he does not come from the past. He has no history. In fact, he has no autobiography. He is so fresh, like a dewdrop—so fresh, just the fresh morning. It has nothing to do with the past. But then you will have to face him, then you will have to look directly.

People come to me. One man came who is a follower of Ramakrishna. He said, "I see Ramakrishna in you." Why? Can't you see me directly? Why see Ramakrishna in me? And I know that if this man was to face Ramakrishna, he would see Ram or Krishna in him, but not Ramakrishna; again, the past.

With the past you feel at ease because it is dead. With dead gods you feel very at ease and comfortable, because they cannot change you, and you can manipulate them. You can put your dead gods anywhere you like. They will not even say, "I don't like this place." They cannot say anything; they cannot assert. They are not there. It is good, comfortably good, conveniently good.

In Jesus you can see Jeremias. Jeremias himself was a very dangerous man. You missed Jeremias; then you were seeing Moses in him. Now Jesus comes. By the time Jeremias is dead, he has become a statue, a fossil. Now his words don't carry any meaning to you; you have listened to them so much, they have lost significance. Now you want to see that fossil in Jesus.

Why can't you see the truth that is facing you? Why do you go on avoiding? Why do you look sideways? Why can't you be immediate? Why can't you see that which is? Why are you obsessed with the past and why do you go on translating the present into the past?

If I say something, immediately your mind starts translating it into the past. You don't listen to me; you listen to your translations. I say something—the Hindu immediately translates it and he says, "Yes, this is what Krishna says in the Gita." The Mohammedan translates it immediately: "Yes, this is what Mohammed says in the Koran." Why can't you listen to *me*? What is the need of bringing the Koran and the Gita in?

No, this is some trick of the mind. If you bring the Gita in, you can avoid me. Then the Gita becomes the barrier. Then you are protected behind a dead Gita; then you need not listen to the song that is happening this moment. Then your ears are filled with the past, your eyes filled with dust. Your being, afraid, is defending itself. This is your armour—the Gita, the Koran, the Vedas, the Talmud—this is your armour. You look *behind* the scriptures. That is a way of not looking. If you want to look really, drop all scriptures, because truth is always fresh and virgin. It has nothing to do with the past.

> *Some say that thou art John the Baptist:*
> *some, Elias; and others, Jeremias,*
> *or one of the prophets.*

There are two types of people who are against. One will say, "You are nothing; just a pretender, a deception, a deceiver."

The other—who does not seem against it—will say, "You represent, you are an incarnation of Krishna, Buddha, Jeremias, Moses." Both are avoiding you—one by denying, one by accepting but not looking at you. Not only are enemies against, sometimes even followers are against. Not only are enemies trying to escape, even friends. Maybe the friend is more cunning —because the enemy simply says *no*. The friend says *yes*, but says it in such a way that it ultimately means *no*. The friend is more cunning.

There is only one way to see Jesus, and that is to see him as he is; directly. No scriptures are needed to interpret him. He has to be seen untranslated. He has to be seen directly—he has to be faced and encountered, eye to eye, heart to heart. Dangerous it is, I know, and risky, because you will never be the same again once you encounter the reality, that which is, the truth.

> *He saith unto them,*
> *But whom say ye that I am?*

Leave people aside. Now he asks his own disciples, "What do *you* think? Whom say ye that I am?" Only one disciple spoke. The eleven remained silent. Nothing is said about them. They must have been puzzled. What to say?—because whenever you say to Jesus, "You are Jeremias," you think you are praising him. You are condemning; you are rejecting. You are not explaining—you are explaining him away.

> *And Simon Peter answered and said . . .*

Only one . . . a very innocent man. Just the other day we were talking about his story; the man of little faith. But at least a little faith was in him, and even if there is a little faith, it can grow. The mustard seed can become a big plant, a big bush, and birds of heaven can shelter in it. Yes, Peter was a man of little faith, but even a little faith is like a spark. It can burn the whole forest. The spark is never little. Even a little spark has tremendous energy, once it starts functioning.

> *And Simon Peter answered and said,*
> *Thou art the Christ,*
> *the Son of the living God.*

Very significant words—try to understand them.

Thou art the Christ. What does this word 'Christ' mean? It has nothing to do with Jesus. Buddha is also a Christ, Krishna is also a Christ. And there is every possibility that the word 'Christ' comes from 'Krishna'. In Bengali, Krishna is called 'Cristo'. There is every possibility that Christ is a form of the same root, Krishna.

What does 'Krishna' mean? The word means 'that which attracts'. Krishna is one who has become capable of attracting the divine in him. Christ is also the same. It means the drop has become capable of attracting the ocean in him. Christ is a meeting-point of the drop with the ocean, of the finite with the infinite, of the horizontal with the vertical. Where the horizontal and the vertical meet, that point of meeting is Christ.

When Simon Peter said, "Thou art the Christ," this is what he meant. He said, "In *you* I can see the finite and the infinite meeting. In *you* I can see the Son of man and the Son of God meeting. In *you* I can see boundaries dissolving, matter and no-matter meeting. In *you* I can see time and eternity meeting, life and death meeting." That is the meaning of Christ: where the opposites meet and become one.

Ordinarily the whole of life is divided into opposites—day and night, summer and winter, morning and evening, birth and death. The point of Christ is the meeting of the opposites, where opposites become complementary and are no more opposites. Christ is a paradox, Christ is a very irrational, illogical point. If you try to understand Christ by logic you will miss—you will have to find some other logic. They call it 'the logic by the side' —not on the main road. The main road is possessed by Aristotle;

he dominates there. If you want to understand Christ you will have to go down some bypath, but not the main road. No, you will never meet Christ on the superhighway. That is possessed by the logicians, the professors, the thinkers, the philosophers. You will have to get down and run into the wilderness.

I am reminded of an old story. It happened: A merchant, very old man, was in heavy debt, and the money-lender was a very dangerous man. The money-lender came to the merchant's house. It must have been a morning like this, a winter morning. The merchant was sitting outside in his small garden. Where he was sitting the garden was paved with white and black pebbles.

His young and beautiful daughter was also sitting by his side. The money-lender had come to threaten that if the man was not going to pay the money within a certain limit of time, he would be thrown into prison for at least twenty years. But he softened a little on looking at the beautiful girl. He proposed. He said, "I know that you cannot pay your debts, and I know that legally you can be thrown into prison for at least twenty years. You are almost seventy; that will be the end of your life. But I am kind and I have always been kind to you. I will give you an opportunity, and this is my proposal: I will take two pebbles, one black and one white, and put them in my bag, and then your daughter has to take one pebble from my bag. If she takes the white pebble out, you are freed of your debt, and nothing happens to your daughter. If she takes the black pebble out, then you are freed of your debt, but your daughter will have to marry me."

Very reluctantly the father and daughter agreed, because there was no other possibility. The money-lender took two pebbles. When he was taking the two pebbles, the old merchant could not see, he was almost filled with tears, but the sharp eyes of the young girl could see that he had taken two black pebbles.

Now, ordinary logic fails. What to do? Two black pebbles in the bag! The obvious thing to do is to expose the fraud, but then he will be annoyed and will take revenge; and the father will be thrown into jail immediately. To annoy him didn't seem to be the right way. Then what to do?—because whatsoever she does, a black pebble will be coming out. Logic fails.

In the West there is one logician, a new type of logician. He calls his logic 'lateral' and his name is de Bono. He quotes this story again and again. And he says that wherever he quotes it he enquires of people, "Now what to do?" And he says that only once did a woman stand up and answer the right thing. But she said at the same time, "My husband thinks that I'm illogical."

What happened? What did the girl do? She didn't expose him; she didn't argue about the fact that he had taken two black pebbles. She withdrew one pebble out of the bag, fumbled, dropped the pebble on the path—it was lost. There were many pebbles and it could not be recognized. Profusely, she wanted to be excused, forgiven. And then she suggested a solution: "Look at the other pebble that is left inside. If it is black, then the one that I withdrew must have been white. If it is white, then the other was black." And the old money-lender could not do anything. The failure was absolute.

This is logic by the side. It is not on the path; it is illogical, it is lateral. You don't go directly, you zig-zag.

If you want to understand Jesus, you will have to go a little zig-zag. He is a paradox—that is the meaning of Christ. In him the opposites meet. That's why he goes on calling himself son of man, and at the same time son of God. Anybody who thinks logically will say that you can say only one thing, not two together. Either you are son of man—then finish, and don't say you are son of God. Or you are son of God, and don't say you are son of man. But he says both, he means both, and he *is* both.

In fact, everybody is both. But you have not looked at yourself, and your mind is caught up in logical patterns. So whatsoever is illogical within you, whatsoever is wild within you, you don't look at it; you simply deny it, you suppress it. That's how the unconscious mind is created.

You have only one mind. Jesus has one mind. I have one mind, but your mind you have divided in two. You have created a boundary. A small space of the mind you call 'mind' and the remainder you have denied. That denied part has become the unconscious, and it takes revenge. It goes on fighting with you. You are split.

All humanity is schizophrenic. Only sometimes is there a man who is not schizophrenic, who is integrated and one. Jesus is one. That is the meaning of 'Christ'. In him, the infinite and the finite meet.

This simple man Simon, also called Peter,

> ... *answered and said,*
> *Thou art the Christ,*
> *the Son of the living God.*

What does this Peter mean when he says, "Son of the living God"? Is there a God who is dead? Yes! Not only is there *a* God, there are a thousand and one gods that are dead. The whole past is dead. If you cling to the past, you cling to dead gods. The living God is always here now, because God has only one time, and that is present. He has no past, no future. People believe in past gods, and people also believe in future gods. Jews who crucified Jesus believed in past incarnations—Moses, Abraham, Ezekiel, all the prophets; and they also believed in a messiah who was to come in the future. And Jesus was there. The future had already come and the past was already fulfilled in him. The past and future were meeting in him, the paradox, the Christ, but they wouldn't see. They are still waiting for a future messiah to come.

Remember, God is never in the past. Past is already dead, and God cannot be dead, so all past gods are dead gods. That means they are not there, they are only in your memory. And there is no future for God. For God, only present exists. From that altitude, from that peak, there is no future—there is only present.

Have you heard about the scientific discovery of the fact that if a watch moves as fast as light, it stops? It is a beautiful phenomenon: time stops itself. And all scriptures say that God is light. At that speed, time stops. There is no past, no future, only the present. The hands of the clock don't move. They remain, they always remain, at the same point.

There is no future God; there is no past God; there is only God as life herenow.

That is the meaning of "the Son of the living God". Christians have been misinterpreting it. They say, "The god of the Hindus is dead, the god of the Jews is dead, the god of the Mohammedans is dead, only the Christian god is alive." They have been misinterpreting the whole thing. No, the Christian god is also dead. The past is dead. Whatsoever become past is dead, and whatsoever is part of the future is not yet born. God is. Is-ness is God, present presence, absolute presence herenow.

> *And Jesus answered and said unto him,*
> *Blessed art thou, Simon Barjona:*
> *for flesh and blood*
> *hath not revealed it unto thee,*
> *but my Father which is in heaven.*

Jesus said, "Blessed art thou, Simon. You are blessed. Because: *for flesh and blood hath not revealed it unto thee.* Because whatsoever you have seen cannot be seen by the eyes of flesh. Whatsoever you have seen cannot be seen by *you.* It is possible only when God reveals it to you; it is possible only when the infinite descends in you, when the grace happens."

You cannot realize God because you are the barrier. You are not there, God realizes himself in you.

Blessed art thou, Simon Barjona:
for flesh and blood
hath not revealed it unto thee,
but my Father which is in heaven.

*O*nce Alexander asked Diogenes, "What do you think about God?"

Diogenes said, "It does not matter what *I* think about God. The only thing that matters is what God thinks about me."

Absolutely true: it does not matter what you think about God. How can it matter? The only thing that matters is what God thinks about you. Your philosophy, your thinking, your doctrines, your creeds, are useless, all rubbish, rot.

Be silent. You need not think about God. When thinking disappears, God starts thinking about you, caring about you, fulfilling you. He comes. He becomes a guest.

And I say also unto thee,
That thou art Peter,
and upon this rock I will build my church;
and the gates of hell
shall not prevail against it.

. . . the man of little faith, but at least of faith. Jesus says, "I will build my church upon your rock, and the gates of hell shall not prevail against it."

Jesus gathered very simple people around him. He was a great master who could see deeply into the possibilities and potentialities.

It is said of Michaelangelo that once he came across a great marble rock which was discarded by the builders. He asked the builders, "Why have you discarded this rock?"

They said, "It is useless."

Michaelangelo laughed and said, "Who told you it is useless?

I can already see an angel waiting to be released in this rock, an angel imprisoned, an imprisoned splendour. Send it to my studio. The angel needs a little help. It is not useless."

No man is useless. Unless you have decided to remain useless, no man is useless. If you allow, as the marble *allows* the artist, the sculptor, to transform it so that the imprisoned splendour can be released, faith—even a little, that will do—is needed. A little trust is needed, and Christ can release in Simon something which can become the rock for his church, for his family, for his community, for those people who are going to love him, and follow him.

> *And I will give unto thee*
> *the keys of the kingdom of heaven:*
> *and whatsoever thou shalt bind on earth*
> *shall be bound in heaven:*
> *and whatsoever thou shalt loose on earth*
> *shall be loosed in heaven.*
>
> *Then charged he his disciples*
> *that they should tell no man*
> *that he was Jesus the Christ.*

... *the key of heaven.* He says, "I will give you the keys of heaven, and whosoever is released on earth by those keys, will remain released in heaven; whosoever is freed on the earth will be free in heaven also, because whatsoever happens on the earth is going to happen in heaven also. Wherever you are right now, you will be there."

And Jesus says, "I will give you keys . . ." What keys? There is only one key in fact, and the key is: how to commit ego suicide, how to commit self-murder, how to become a no-self, how to be, and at the same time be without the 'I'. That is the only key and all other keys are just supportive; all other keys are just supports for the main and basic thing—how to be egoless. And the door opens. . . .

have heard a story that when Jesus died and reached heaven, the angel Gabriel met him at the gate and asked, "What plans do you have, so that the work you have started can be continued on earth?"

Jesus said, "I have left twelve men and a few women who are going to spread my message till it reaches to every heart, to every mind, on the earth."

The angel said, "And if they fail you, have you made other plans also?"

Jesus smiled and said, "I am counting on them. I have no other plan."

Counting on love, counting on these simple villagers— counting on them: there is no other plan, there cannot be.

Meditation is the key. Egolessness is the key, and love is the only plan to spread it all over the earth.

I am also counting on you, on your love, on your trust, on your courage. I am also giving you the key. Don't use it only for yourself— use it first for yourself, then spread the message; because everybody is imprisoned in a rock and everybody needs to be released.

> Then charged he his disciples
> that they should tell no man
> that he was Jesus the Christ.

Why? Because these things are revealed in trust and cannot be told to others. These things are revealed in love.

You call me Bhagwan. That is because of your love. It can be revealed to you. When you talk to others, don't tell it to them. That will offend them and it will be pointless. They will start arguing about it.

You love me. Through your love you have seen something which they cannot see, unless they also love.

Jesus said, "Don't tell them. You have realized the truth. You have seen the vertical in me, but don't go on telling it to

others. They will not understand. They will misunderstand.
They will be offended: because that which is known through
love can only be understood through love."

4   Surrender is the door to bliss, to beauty, to truth, to love, to life, to God.

*How would you describe your particular path to en-
lightenment in relationship to other traditional paths
such as the various kinds of Yoga, Sufism, Buddhism,
Zen, Christianity, etcetera?*

I HAVE NO particular path. I don't belong to any path whatsoever, and therefore all paths belong to me. Each path is perfect in itself, but each path can help only a very minor part
of humanity. Each path exists for a particular type. It is complete
in itself. Nothing is to be added to it—nothing is to be deducted
from it. As it is, it is perfect. But it can help only a particular
type. Humanity is vast; one path cannot carry the whole of
humanity. All paths are needed. In fact, as the human mind
changes, more new paths have to be evolved. With the mind
changing, many old paths have become by and by useless, or can
be used only by a very few individuals.

I use all paths. Whenever I see a seeker, I start looking into
him—what type he is and what type of path will be helpful to

him. I may not use the name of the path, because those names have become too much loaded. If a Hindu comes to me and I say to him, "Sufism is your path," he will not be able to understand; he will be immediately closed to it. A Hindu cannot conceive himself on the path of Mohammedans—that's impossible for him.

I will not talk about Sufism, but whatsoever I will give him will be Sufism. To me the path is not important, but the seeker. Paths exist for you, not vice versa. You don't exist for any path or any doctrine. All doctrines, all paths, all dogmas, exist for you. If they are helpful, good; if they are not helpful, they have to be thrown on to the rubbish heap.

Man is important, because man carries the potentiality of being God. Paths are just means. Use them, but don't be used by them. Remain masters, and always remember that you are the end and nothing else is more important than you, than your innermost core. If you remember this, you can use many paths and you can be enriched by many ways.

And this is my understanding, that the more you travel, the more you walk on many paths, the more open you become, the more enriched you are. The whole past of humanity belongs to you. If you are a Mohammedan, don't say that only Mohammed belongs to you—Buddha is also yours, Christ also. The whole past of humanity is your heritage. Why be poor? Why say, "I am a Hindu and only Krishna belongs to me and Christ is a stranger. I won't allow him in my house; only Krishna is allowed"? If only Krishna is allowed, then you will have only one door to your house, only one room to your house—then you cannot be multi-dimensional. But if Christ also comes, and Mohammed is also welcomed, then you will have an enrichment; then you have different flowers in your garden; then you will have many types of diamonds in your treasury.

Don't confine yourself. Remain open. Welcome everything that has happened on the earth, and that all is yours. Claim it, and use whatsoever you can use for your own growth. Don't stick and don't cling, otherwise you will be frozen. My whole effort here is to melt you, so that you can start flowing in many currents.

You are frozen. Somebody is a frozen Christian. Somebody is a frozen Hindu. Somebody is a frozen Jain. Somebody is a frozen Buddhist—all dead. Melt! Become a little warmer! You have become so cold and so closed. Become warm. Allow the sun's rays to work on you.

And don't protect yourself. Become vulnerable. Melt in a thousand and one currents—unafraid and fearless, start flowing. God comes through a thousand and one ways. And if he comes through a thousand and one ways, let him come that way—let yourself be introduced to God through as many possibilities as possible. Why cling to one form? Why cling to one name? All names are his and all forms are his. And the more you become acquainted that all forms are his, the more possibility there is that you will become aware that he is formless. Otherwise, how can all forms be his? Only the formless can manifest itself in millions of forms. Only the pathless can be travelled through so many paths, and only the gateless can be achieved through so many gates.

Don't be poor. Become rich, and claim the whole heritage of man! That's why I go on talking of Christ, Mahavir, Krishna, Patanjali, Buddha, Zarathustra, Lao Tzu. This is nothing but to show you that the whole of humanity is yours. You are vast! You are not frozen dead particles—you are alive beings, and life is infinite.

I have no particular path. All paths are mine. I am not concerned with paths—I am concerned with you. I look into you because you are important; you are the goal, and nothing else matters. Then I decide what will be suitable for you. Sometimes one path is suitable for you, sometimes two, sometimes three, sometimes many. It depends how you have grown in your past lives. You may once have been a Mohammedan and you worked a little on that path; you progressed a little on that way. Then you became a Christian, and you worked on that path a little. Then you became a Buddhist. You have lived so many lives. You have forgotten them—I cannot forget them. You can be forgiven if you forget. I cannot be forgiven if I forget.

When I look into you, I don't look only into your present because in your present all your past is involved: it is there in its totality, layer upon layer; you are an infinite territory . . . when I look into you, I look at how many ways you have been working upon yourself, a little on this path, a little on that. Then both of the paths will be helpful to you; then in you already a synthesis has happened.

I'm not for synthesis, for any artificial combination—I'm not in favour of it. I'm not in favour of synthesizing Christianity with Hinduism, but what can I do? I am helpless; it has happened in you. You have been once a Mohammedan, then a Hindu, then a Christian. What can I do? It is in your blood, in your consciousness; the synthesis has already happened. I'm not trying to synthesize, but for you a synthetic path in which all the three are involved, will be helpful. It will give you a sudden surge of energy—it will release something within you. You will start flowering in many directions immediately, and many flowers are to come. . . .

When I see that a man has been consistently following one path, then there is no need for synthesis; then he has to follow that path. If one has been for at least seven lives a Buddhist, then there is no need—then it will be confusing for him to give him something else. He has already worked hard on a particular path; now he has to be helped on the same path.

So when *you* come to me, if you are a Buddhist and you have been a Buddhist in your past lives, I am here to make you a greater Buddhist. If you come to me and you have been a Christian in your past lives, I am here to make you a greater

Christian. I may not tell you that I am helping you to be a Christian, but don't be deceived by the appearances. I may not be saying that I am helping you to be a Buddhist, but I am doing that. One day when the light will dawn on you, then you will suddenly realize that I was not a detractor. I have not taken you on another path which you were not on—I have simply helped you on the same path, because all paths are mine. No particular path is mine. In that way I am richer than anybody else who has ever existed in the world. They had particular paths. The same Christ cannot say to you what I am saying. And the same Mahavir cannot say to you what I am saying. They had particular paths— I have none. I claim the whole of humanity.

What is the difference between being a fatalist and just floating, feeling everything is beautiful?

A vast difference, a lot of difference. And the difference is not of quantity, the difference is of quality. The fatalist is one who has not understood life, but who has felt failure. A fatalist is one who feels helpless, frustrated. In fatalism he seeks consolation. He says, "It was going to be so." He's trying to avoid that he has failed. It was going to be so, so what can he do? He is throwing the responsibility on fate, on God, on XYZ. "I'm not responsible, what can I do? It was written in my fate. It was predetermined, predestined." He is saying, "I'm not responsible." He has failed. In deep frustration he is trying to find some refuge, some shelter. Fatalism is a consolation.

And the other thing, 'just floating, feeling everything is beautiful', is not a consolation—it is an understanding. It is not fatalism; it is not failure; it is not helplessness. It is simply a deep insight into reality, as things are. It is to understand that you are a very small part of the cosmic whole. And you are not separate. You are one with the continent—you are not an island.

The understanding that the ego is false, the understanding that the separation is false, the understanding that you don't have a separate destiny than the whole, that a drop in the ocean need not worry about its own destiny—the ocean has to worry about it—is not helplessness. In fact it releases tremendous power. Once you are unburdened by yourself, once you are no more worried about yourself, you become a tremendous energy. Then the energy is no more struggling; now it floats. Now you are not fighting with the whole, now you are with the whole, marching with the whole. Then you are not trying to prove anything against the whole, because that is simply foolish.

It is as if my own hand starts fighting with me and starts trying to have its own destiny, separate from me. I am going to the south, and my head starts going to the north. It is so foolish, it is impossible—foolish, and impossible—and frustration is bound to be there. Sooner or later the hand will see that the hand wanted to go to the north, but it is going to the south. Deep in frustration, the hand will say, "It is fate. I am helpless."

In fact, the feeling of helplessness arises because of the struggle. When you understand that you are part of the whole, that you are not separate at all, that in fact the whole has been trying to attain some heights through you; you are only a passage, a vehicle—suddenly all frustration disappears. When you don't have a goal of your own, how can you be frustrated? When you don't have to prove anything against anything; when you don't have to struggle, there is no need for fatalism; you need not have any consolation. You simply dance with the whole; you flow with the whole. You know you *are* the whole.

That is the meaning when the Upanishads say: *Aham Brahmasmi*—I am God. That is the meaning when Jesus says, "I and my God are one"—not fatalism, not settling in helplessness; rather, knowing the fact that we are one with the whole. Then

•

your atomic tinyness disappears. You become cosmic.

. . . *just floating, feeling everything is beautiful.* Then it happens; then you just float; there is nothing else to do. The same energy that was trying to fight, surrenders. Then you are not pushing the river: you simply float on the river, and the river takes you. The river is already going to the ocean. You are unnecessarily worried. You can simply leave that responsibility to the river. Whether you leave it or not, it is already going.

Don't fight, because in fight there is going to be frustration— in fight is the seed of frustration, and in frustration you will seek some way to console yourself. Then fatalism is born.

If you don't fight then everything is just beautiful. Why? Because then you don't have any idea of your own to compare it with. Everything is beautiful for how could it be otherwise? You don't have any conflict; hence everything is beautiful. If the river turns to the right, you turn to the right—beautiful. If the river turns to the left—perfectly beautiful, you turn to the left. If you have some idea and some goal, if you say, "I am a leftist," then there is going to be trouble. When the river starts turning towards the right, you will say, "Now this is going too far; now I cannot surrender—I am a leftist." Then you will start fighting against the river, and then the river will not be beautiful because your notion, your idea, your ideal, has come in.

Whenever ideology comes in, things become ugly. All idealists live in hells. Ideology creates hells. If you don't have any ideology you have nothing to compare: you don't have any criterion. Then whatsoever is happening, is happening—you have nothing to compare it with. Then wherever the river is going, that is the only way to go. Then one simply allows existence to have its own way. One never comes in the way; a deep let-go.

Then everything is beautiful. And then you realize that it has never been otherwise. Everything was beautiful, always. Look at the animals; look at the birds; look at the clouds; look at the trees. Ask the trees; ask the stones. Everything is beautiful. The trees must be very much surprised that you look so sad. The trees must be puzzled that man looks so burdened, when everything is so light and so floating. The birds must be laughing at you that you go on carrying such a load—the load seems to be nowhere except in your mind.

So much burdened, you miss life. So much burdened, you miss love. So much burdened, you miss celebration. So much burdened, you miss laughter. You cannot sing; you cannot dance; you cannot laugh. And because of this, you become desperate and you start fighting more. You think you are not fighting as much as you should. That's why you are not so happy.

Once a man came to me, a very rich man, but very reluctant to accept the fact that he was not happy. People don't accept that they are not happy. They *are* unhappy, but they won't accept it because that is very ego shattering. They, and unhappy? Impossible.

I looked into that rich man. I see thousands of unhappy men, but he was rare—I have not found another so unhappy. And he had everything. And he tried to smile. The smile was absolutely false, painted, just on the lips, not coming from anywhere; not coming from the inner being; just mentally created, a facade, a trick of the mind. I immediately looked at the man and felt that he was so unhappy, but also unable to accept being unhappy. So I said to the man, "You look so happy. What are the reasons for your happiness?"

He looked surprised. He was never expecting that. He said, "What do you say—I, and happy?"

"Yes, I have never seen such a happy man. And that's why I would like—enlighten me a little—what are the causes of your happiness?"

The man started enumerating, "I have so much money, a beautiful wife, children, palaces, cars, swimming pools, this and that." But while he was enumerating, deep down, there was only hell and darkness. And he knew it, and he could not believe that he had deceived me. But still he was trying.

Then I asked one question more: "You say that because of these things you are happy; just one question more. You say that you are happy. I would like to know, how much happiness has your happiness given you? How much happiness has your happiness really given you?"

Then he caught the point. He started crying and he said, "I am not happy. And you have caught me. I go on deceiving myself that I am happy. I go on deceiving others. I am desperate to prove that I am happy."

Remember, only an unhappy man tries to prove that he is happy; only a sad man tries to prove that he is not sad; only a dead man tries to prove that he is alive; only a coward tries to prove that he is brave. Only a man who knows his inferiority tries to prove that he is superior. You go on trying to prove the opposite of what you are, and the possibilities are ninety-nine out of a hundred that you are just the opposite. When you smile, I can see hidden tears. When you try to dance, I can see the rock-like heart within that cannot move. Dancing is impossible.

*W*hy is man in such a plight? The whole world laughs. The trees laugh at you. You may not hear; you may be escaping; you may have become deaf. The birds laugh; the animals laugh. Something has gone wrong with man. What has gone wrong with him? Only one thing: the whole of nature is flowing and man is fighting. In nature the ego does not exist. Trees are there, but without any egos—only man is with the ego. And that ego is the whole hell.

That ego needs continuous fight, because it feeds on fight. The more you fight, the stronger your ego becomes. It is a fighter. That's why surrender is so difficult. But unless you

surrender you will remain in misery. Surrender is the door to
bliss, to beauty, to truth, to love, to life, to God. Surrender is the
door. And when I say 'surrender', I don't mean that surrender
has to be towards someone. That is just an excuse; because you
cannot surrender unless you have someone to surrender to—
that's why someone is needed. Otherwise there is no need; you
can simply surrender, and the door is open.

That's what Buddha says. He said, "Simply surrender." But
that looks very difficult for the mind. You need some excuse.
Jesus says, "Surrender to God." If you cannot just surrender,
then surrender to God. Krishna says, "If you cannot surrender,
then surrender to me. Let me be the excuse." But when you
surrender, then you know that Krishna tricked you. When you
surrender you will not find Krishna there: you will find the whole
cosmos and you floating in it, part of it. Then you are no more
separate—not going on *your* way. Then everything is beautiful,
blissful. Without conflict ugliness disappears; without conflict
sadness disappears; without conflict sorrow disappears. Then
whatsoever is, is beautiful.

And it is so. But it is not fatalism. It is not an 'ism' at all. It
has nothing to do with a faith or predetermination or any nonsense. It has simply something to do with the insight that I
belong to the whole and the whole belongs to me; that I am
in my home, I am not a stranger. And there is no need to fight.

With whom are you fighting? All fight is foolish, is stupid.
Surrender is wisdom. Fight is stupid. Float; flow with the flow;
move with the whole. Don't have private dreams and don't
have private goals. Don't have a private ideology. Then this
moment you live; and when the next moment comes, you live
in it. If life is there, you live life; if death comes, you live death.
Whatsoever happens, you are grateful.

I have heard about a Sufi mystic who used to pray and every
day thank God. His disciples were worried. Many times they
were very much puzzled, because sometimes it was okay to

thank God because things were going well. But the man was absolutely unconcerned about things—sometimes when things were going very badly, then too he would give thanks.

One day it was too much: the disciples for three days were hungry and starving, and they were not given refuge in any town. They were thrown out. The people were very orthodox, and the master was a revolutionary, a very unorthodox, non-traditional man, unconventional, nonconformist; so no village would allow them even to have shelter in the night. And they were without food. On the fourth day, in the morning, when the master started praying, the disciples said, "Now it is going too far—he said to God, 'How wonderful you are! You always give me whatsoever I need.' "

Then one disciple said, "Wait, one minute. Now it is becoming absurd. What are you saying? Three days we have been hungry. We are dying; no shelter in any town, and you are thanking God that whatsoever you need he always gives!"

And the mystic started laughing, and he said, "Yes, for these three days we needed starvation; for these three days we needed to be rejected. He always gives whatsoever we need. For these three days we needed to be poor, absolutely poor. Whatsoever we need he always gives, and I am thankful." And he started praying and thanking God and being grateful.

If you are not fighting, then an understanding arises that everything is beautiful and whatsoever is needed is happening, whatsoever is needed for your growth. Sometimes poverty is needed; sometimes starvation is needed; sometimes illness is needed. In fact, I have not come across anything which is not a need sometimes to someone. If you understand, you accept. If you accept, you grow. If you reject, your whole energy becomes a wastage in fighting. The same situation could have been a growth—now it is simply a wastage, a leakage.

Don't be a fatalist, because in the first place don't fight. If you fight and get frustrated, then fatalism enters in. In the first place, don't fight.

One man came to me and he was in much trouble because he got married and he found a woman, as almost all people find, a very quarrelsome woman, continuously fighting and creating hell for him. He came to me and said, "Have compassion on me." And he said, "I would like to ask one question. What would you have done in my place?"

I told him, "In the first place I would not have been in your place! Why should I be?"

A man who is floating, accepting, understanding, has no need of fatalism. In the first place he is not fighting, so there is no need to seek some consolation.

Fatalism is the end of a wrong life, and the feeling of let-go is the beginning of a right life. They are vastly different, tremendously different, qualitatively different. Remember the difference, because it happens that you would also like to say good things about your failures. When you fail, you start saying, "Now I am in a let-go." Don't try to deceive yourself, because you are deceiving only yourself; the existence is not deceived. If you have failed, try to understand why you have failed. In the first place you started fighting, that's why.

If you understand that, then even your successes will look like failures. They are. Sooner or later each success becomes a failure. It is only a question of time. What you call success is failure on the way.

So if every man is given enough time to fight then success and failure will all disappear and everybody will become a fatalist. That's why in old conditions, ancient conditions, fatalism exists—not in new countries. For example, in America fatalism does not exist. It is a child country, a baby country, just three hundred years of history; it is nothing. In India, fatalism exists:

thousands and thousands of years of history, so old and so ancient that it has known all success, all failure; it has known all types of frustration. Now, finding no other way, it seeks consolation in fatalism.

As a country grows old, it becomes fatalist. As a man grows old, he becomes a fatalist. Young people are not fatalists: they believe in themselves. Old people become fatalists, because by that time they have come to know at least one thing, that they have failed. Then they find consolation.

The whole basis is wrong. In the first place don't fight, then there will be no need to fail; there will be no need to succeed; there will be no need to fight and there will be no need to console yourself. Each moment is such a blessing if you don't fight.

As an artist, I tend to claim my perceptions, desiring recognition for sharing my visions with others. My ego is strong. How can the Western artist be free of ego and transcend the dichotomy of the aesthetic and the spiritual?

First, there is no dichotomy between the aesthetic and the spiritual. The aesthetic is spiritual in the seed form; there is no dichotomy. The same sensitivity grows into spirituality. If you cannot see beauty, you will be absolutely incapable of seeing God. If you can see beauty, then you are approaching near God; the temple is coming closer. You may not be fully aware, but you are on the way. You have heard the first note of that music. Maybe you cannot yet recognize it; it is vague, but you have seen the first glimpse of the sun. Maybe it is too much clouded.

Beauty is the first glimpse of the divine. Wherever you see

beauty, remember you are on holy ground. Wherever, I say:
in a human face, in a child's eyes, in a lotus flower, or in the
wings of a bird in flight, in the rainbow, or in a silent rock.
Wherever you see beauty, remember, you are on holy ground
—God is close. Beauty is the first glimpse of the divine; so there
is no dichotomy between beauty and truth. The aesthetic and the
spiritual are not two things, two points on the same path, two
milestones on the same pilgrimage.

But the so-called religions have created a dichotomy. They
have created a dichotomy and they have poisoned the whole
mind of humanity. The so-called religions are afraid of beauty
because somehow, in beauty they feel sex hidden. That becomes
the trouble. Wherever they feel beauty they feel the erotic, and
they have been thinking that the erotic is against the divine. It
is not. The erotic is the first glimpse of the divine. It is not the
last; that has to be remembered. But it is the first arising of the
same energy. The energy is the same; it is the first flood; it is
the first tremor, but the energy is the same. If the energy goes
higher and higher and higher, then it becomes a great wave of
bliss; then it reaches to the heavens.

Because religions became afraid of sex, because they became
afraid of the body, they became afraid of beauty: because beauty
is form. God is formless. Beauty is form, but the form is of the
formless. Because religions became afraid of the world, they
started thinking of God as against the world—this is some
absurdity that entered into all religions. They all say that God
created the world, and at the same time they say that you cannot
attain to God if you don't renounce the world. This is patent
foolishness, because if the world is God's creation, then why
should it be a basic requirement to renounce it? Rather, one
would think that the basic requirement should be that one should
rejoice in it. It is God's creation. If you love the painter, you love
his paintings also. In fact, you come to know the painter only
through his paintings; there is no other way. If you love the

poet, you love his poetry also. How do you know that he is a poet? It is only through his poetry. No poet will say that you can love him only if you renounce his poetry.

If God is the creator, then the world has to be loved, loved totally, loved deeply. You have to get involved in it: rejoice in it, delight in it. Only through your delight will you by and by have glimpses of the creator in the creation. If you look at the painting of a great painter, you will have glimpses of the master. It cannot be otherwise, because the master has come into those colours; his touch is there, the master touch. If you love the poetry and you penetrate into it, you will find the heart of the poet beating there. And unless you have penetrated that depth, you have not understood, you cannot understand it. Unless the poetry becomes the heart of the poet, it is not understood.

The world has to be rejoiced. The body is beautiful—delight in it. It is a gift of God. Don't try to renounce it, because renouncing it means you reject the master.

Gurdjieff used to say that all religions are against God, and he is perfectly right. The so-called religions are all against God. They talk about God, but they are against God. They show it through their actions. They say, "Renounce the world, renounce the body."

'Renounce' should be a dirty word. Rejoice! Replace 're-nounce' by 'rejoice' and a totally different conception of religion arises. Then aesthetics, then beauty, then the sensitivity to beauty is not against spirituality. Then it becomes the beginning.

And one has to deepen it. Be committed to beauty, and through it you will come to know what religions call 'God'; you will come to know divinity, divineness.

So this is the first thing, that there is no dichotomy between aesthetics and spirituality, between poetry and religion, between body and spirit, between the world and God. There is no dichotomy. The world is God become visible. Poetry is the poet expressed. Painting is the painter in form. The formless has descended into the form, but there is no dichotomy, there is no duality and there is no antagonism.

Second thing: *As an artist I tend to claim my perceptions, desiring recognition for sharing my visions with others.* Sharing is beautiful, but seeking recognition is not so beautiful. In fact, both cannot exist together—they are antagonistic. If you want, if you are desiring recognition, then you don't want to share really. You share as a means to be recognized. Then your painting or your poetry or your dance is just a means to fulfil the ego. That will make you separate from the whole. The ego is the separation. Then your whole life will become ugly, and how, out of an ugly life, can beauty be born? Impossible.

If you are beautiful deep within you, only then can the beauty flow from you. Only out of a beautiful life, a beautiful painting is born. There is no other way. *You* are flowing into your painting, into your work of art, into your sculpture, into your music, into your poetry. It is coming from you. It brings you; it is your consciousness flowing. If it is only to gain recognition, then you are ugly. The ego is ugly because it is a separation from the whole, because it is false. You are not separate.

The untruth cannot be beautiful, remember. Truth is beauty. The untrue, the lie, cannot be beautiful. It is ugly—they are synonymous. The ego is the moss untrue thing in the world. It only seems to exist, it doesn't exist, it is a false phenomenon. And if you are seeking recognition, then you are seeking the ego and you are trying to fulfil a false thing. Out of this ugliness, beauty cannot flow—out of ugliness, only ugliness is possible.

And if you are trying to fulfil the ego you are not interested in sharing, because sharing is an act of love. Not that there will not be recognition if you share—but that is not the point. In fact if you share, much recognition will happen, but you are not seeking it; you were not after it. If it happens it is okay; if it doesn't happen it is the same. You want to share. Your happiness is in sharing, not in the after-effects of it; not in the result, not in the end, but in the act itself.

For example, you love a man or a woman. While you love, you hold hands or you embrace each other. The very act in itself is the end, not that you are trying to prove that you are a man; not that the woman later on says to you that you are a great lover. If you love a woman just to hear from her that you are a great lover, you have not loved her at all. But if you love a woman, who bothers what she says? What she feels in the moment of sharing is the thing, is the real thing; it is enough unto itself.

If a woman loves a man and she loves only as a means, so that the man can say later on, "How beautiful you are," she is seeking recognition for her beauty. That is an ego effort, an ego trip, but there is no love in it. And she cannot be beautiful.

If she loves and shares her being, in that sharing she is beautiful. There is no need even to say, "You are beautiful." If someone says it, okay; if somebody doesn't say it, that doesn't mean that it has not been said, because there are deeper ways to say things. Sometimes to remain silent is the only way to speak.

I have heard, that in one museum in Europe, there is a piano on which Wagner used to play. A woman came there to see it, and she was just a learner, just knowing only the ABC of it. She immediately started playing on the piano. The guide was shocked, but he was a very polite man, so he remained silent. After a few strokes, the woman said that many great musicians must have come to the museum to see this piano of Wagner, and they all must have played on it.

The guide said, "Madam, you are the first. Great musicians come here. They stand absolutely silent. And I have heard them say, 'We are not worthy even to touch it.' They remain in silence; they don't utter a single word. The moment they see this, the master's piano, it is as if they become dumb. They don't touch it. They say, 'We are not worthy of it.' In their deep silence, they say something."

When you love a woman, in deep silence much is said. When somebody comes to see a painting, if he starts chattering about it, that simply shows he has not been in deep rapport with it; otherwise the chattering would stop. If he starts saying something about it, that shows that he is trying to show his knowledge about paintings. Otherwise, before a great painting one becomes silent, one has nothing to say. Language is lost; one becomes dumb. The mind stops.

When you love a person, you share; you don't ask for recognition. If you ask for recognition, you don't share, you don't want to share. Your sharing is just an empty gesture, just a means to recognition. It is not love; it is prostitution. A great artist does not bother about recognition. He loves his art, his work. He loves to share it, but he's not asking for anything; it is unconditional sharing: and then it has tremendous beauty. That is the difference between great art and mediocre art, and that is the difference between Eastern art and Western art.

Go to the great Eastern temples. Go to Khajuraho or to Ellora, Ajanta—tremendously beautiful works, but you don't even know who has made them; they have not even signed them. What of recognition? Nobody knows; they are anonymous. Nobody knows who has written the Upanishads—anonymous. But they shared; they are still sharing and they will go on sharing to the very end of time. Whenever you go to Khajuraho, your mind will stop. Such tremendous beauty has never been revealed anywhere in the world. Stones have never been so expressive as in Khajuraho, sermons in stones. Even real women have never been so beautiful as the Khajuraho sculpture. And to bring it into stone . . . such subtle, euphoric feelings, like two lovers making love!—what happens to their faces, what type of energy surrounds them, what ecstasy travels between them—in stone, the hardest medium! But they have depicted even the ecstasy. When two lovers make love, what type of energy surrounds them— even that energy they have brought to those stones; it surrounds them still.

Looking at those faces, you can see that they are not only erotic. The erotic is just the beginning, the first rung of the ladder. If you have insight you will see the ladder going higher and higher, and then it disappears into the clouds. Somewhere in the clouds the ecstasy is there. But nobody knows who made those beautiful images. Anonymous—but they shared. And one still feels grateful and will always feel grateful.

Eastern art is anonymous and hence its beauty—it is as if of the other world. Western art, particularly the modern, not the classical, is too much egoistic. Even a Picasso is too much egoistic. He may be a great painter, a great master, but neurotic all the same; a great genius, but gone astray, neurotic. He's mad. His madness may have a method, that's another thing, but he is mad. And the whole madness is because of the ego. Whatsoever he has painted, great works, but the neurosis is there.

And if you look and meditate on Picasso's paintings long enough, you will feel restless, uneasy. Something of the neurosis will start happening in you also, something of the quality of nightmare. Don't keep Picasso's paintings in your bedrooms; otherwise you will have nightmares! Have a small Buddha, by some anonymous sculptor. That will surround your sleep; that will protect your sleep; that will give you a subtle awareness even while you are asleep.

So, sharing is one thing, and asking for recognition is totally another. Share; don't ask for recognition. I'm not saying that recognition will not come—it will come profusely. Ask for recognition and it won't come so profusely. Even if it comes, it will limp. Because when *you* ask for recognition, the other becomes reluctant to give it. Because when *you* are seeking your ego, the other also wants to seek his own ego. Then you provoke criticism rather than recognition. And the one who recognizes your art is deep down recognizing, through his recognition, his own recognition. So you say that you are a great lover of art—then the ego game. Then the beauty is lost; two lies trying to prove themselves to be true.

Share. Recognition will come; it always comes, like a shadow. Don't be bothered by it. Only small mediocre minds are bothered by it.

And the third thing: you say, "My ego is strong." If it is really strong then you can surrender. Only weaklings cannot surrender. To surrender, you need tremendous energy of will. Only a very mature ego can surrender; just as a ripe fruit falls, not an unripe. An unripe fruit cannot fall; you have to force it. A ripe fruit falls of its own accord, so easily that the tree does not even become aware that it has fallen. It falls so naturally.

If the ego is strong, then you can surrender. This is the only thing in favour of the Western mind—that people are being taught to be egoistic. The whole Western psychology has been teaching them to have ripe, mature egos. That is a beautiful thing—dangerous, if one remains clinging to the ego, but with tremendous possibilities. If one really becomes strong in the ego, then surrender is possible.

The Western mind is more egoistic. Surrender seems difficult. The Eastern mind is more humble. Surrender seems easy. But these are appearances. The Eastern mind can surrender very easily, but the surrender is impotent, because you don't have anything to surrender. The ego which has to be surrendered, is not there. It is just like an impotent man taking a vow of celibacy, or a poor man renouncing the kingdom—it is meaningless.

For the Western mind surrender is difficult but meaningful

It will take a long time and a long struggle for the Western mind to surrender, but once the Western mind surrenders, then there is nothing like it. The Eastern mind has to be brought up; the ego has to be ripened and matured. Only at a certain point of maturity, where the ego feels too heavy, the surrender is possible.

The Eastern mind is so humble. It goes on surrendering everywhere and anywhere; it goes on touching everybody's and anybody's feet. The whole thing has become useless; it has become just a mannerism, an etiquette. But when a Western mind bows down and touches somebody's feet, it has significance; otherwise he would not have done it. It is not just a mannerism; it has happened. Something deep has been touched and stirred.

So if you say, "The ego is strong," then prove it! That is the only way. Surrender; that is the only way to prove it. Otherwise I will say it is still weak.

I am so confused. I want to perfect myself, but have lost all idea what effort to make in what way. Your presence makes me want to let go, but much else urges me toward a desperate programme of self-renewal. What can I do?

Perfectionism is a neurosis. It is an illness. And the more you try to become perfect, the more frustrated you will become. The goal of perfection has led the whole of humanity towards madness; the earth has almost become a madhouse.

I don't teach perfection. What do I teach? I teach wholeness, not perfection. Be whole; be total; but don't think about perfection.

Be whole. Whatsoever you do, do it totally. What is the

difference? When you do it totally you are not worried about the result. You did it totally. You are finished. More you could not do. You are not holding anything; you have put all your energy in it, you were whole in it. Now if you fail, you fail. If you succeed, you succeed. But whether you fail or you succeed, you are fulfilled all the same. A deep contentment arises because you have done whatsoever you could do.

You can never be perfect. How can the part be perfect? You can never be perfect. Whatsoever you do, you can always imagine that it could have been better—whatsoever you do, you can imagine that better could have been done.

I have heard about a great painter. He was seventy years old, and one day he finished his painting and started crying and weeping. His disciples surrounded the master and said, "Master, why are you crying? What has happened?"

The master said, "I cannot see any imperfection in this painting. It seems I am dead, finished. It seems I have lost my imagination; that's why I'm crying. This is the first time I cannot see any defect in my painting. I must have lost my imagination."

*W*hatsoever you do, you can always imagine better. So a perfectionist is always in misery. He can never be satisfied, never; that is not for him.

I want you to be whole. Whatsoever you do, you do totally and you are not concerned with the result. You are only concerned that you are not withholding anything. You love; you love totally. You meditate; you meditate totally. You dance; you dance totally. You just become the dance and forget the dancer completely. Whether the dance was perfect or not is not the question at all. And who is to decide? Only one thing you have to decide—whether you were totally in it or not. If you were totally in it, I say it is perfect—if you were not totally in it, I say it is imperfect. That is my meaning of perfection.

It is not comparative. If you dance, you may not dance like Udaya Shanker. Comparatively your dance may be poorer than Udaya Shanker's. But there is a possibility you may be more total in it than Udaya Shanker himself in his dance. Then I say you are more perfect: because it is not a question of form; it is a question of your inner involvement. If the ego drops, then it is whole, then it is total.

I have heard that there was a man in Socrates' time—his name was Alcibiades. He was a perfectionist and of course, he was the most miserable man. Always worried, because everything is going wrong. He was very rich; he could purchase anything. But he wasn't happy because there was always something else to be purchased, something else to be brought to his treasury. He travelled all over the world, but whenever he would come back to Athens he was more miserable than before.

He came to see Socrates and he asked Socrates, "Why am I so miserable?—and I have travelled all over the world. I am the most travelled man in Athens, and one would think that travelling gives experience and maturity. But nothing like that has happened to me. I have become more and more miserable. And I go to the far-off countries and then come back, from India, from China, but I'm not gaining any experience. I am becoming more and more imperfect day by day, rather than becoming perfect. What is the trouble with me?"

Socrates said, "Because you take yourself always with yourself. Wherever you go you take yourself with yourself; that is the trouble. This time you go alone. Leave yourself in Athens. Then there is a possibility of maturity."

If you drop the ego, there is a possibility you may become whole. The moment you become whole, you become holy. Then you are healed; then all wounds disappear. Then you are perfect in your total aloneness. It is not comparative—that you are more perfect than others. No. You are simply perfect; you are a unique piece; there is nobody else like you; you are only like yourself.

In your wholeness you are perfect, and a deep contentment comes. It becomes a climate around you.

The last question, and very important:

> *You are so sweet and rare that I*
> *feel like kidnapping you before I*
> *leave Poona. What do you say?*

I surrender.

MATTHEW 21

12   And Jesus went into the temple of God,
      and cast out
      all them that sold and bought in the temple,
      and overthrew
      the tables of the money-changers,
      and the seats of them that sold doves,

13   And said unto them,
      It is written, My house
      shall be called the house of prayer;
      but ye have made it a den of thieves.

23   And when he was come into the temple,
      the chief priests
      and the elders of the people
      came unto him as he was teaching, and said,
      By what authority doest thou these things?
      and who gave thee this authority?

24 And Jesus answered and said unto them . . .

28 . . . A certain man had two sons;
and he came to the first, and said,
Son, go work today in my vineyard.

29 He answered and said, I will not:
but afterward he repented, and went.

30 And he came to the second,
and said likewise.
And he answered and said, I go, sir:
and went not.

31 Whether of them twain
did the will of his father?
They say unto him, The first.
Jesus saith unto them,
Verily I say unto you,
That the publicans and the harlots
go into the kingdom of God before you.

45 And when the chief priests and the Pharisees
had heard his parables,
they perceived that he spake of them.

46 But when they sought to lay hands on him,
they feared the multitude,
because they took him for a prophet.

5 *No man has ever found God. Whenever man is ready,
God finds him.*

ALL REVOLUTIONS have failed. And when I say 'all', I mean
all. The very concept of revolution proved absolutely
futile, a mirage. Revolution means a rebellion organized.
But you cannot organize a rebellion—that's impossible—because
in the very organization, the rebellion dies. Organization is against
rebellion; so all revolutions fail because they try to succeed. To
be successful they have to be organized. The moment they are
organized they become another establishment. They may be
anti-establishment but still, they have their own establishment.
They cannot be non-establishment—that is impossible. Organize
a revolution and you have killed it. An organized revolution is
aborted already.

Rebellion is unorganized, rebellion is individual. It comes out
of the authenticity of a single being; it comes out of the authenticity of a single being's heart. Revolution is political, rebellion
is religious. Revolution means a social phenomenon; rebellion
is meditative. This has to be understood, this distinction. It is
very significant. And if you miss it, you will miss the very meaning of the life of Jesus, because he is a rebel—he is not a revolu-

tionary. Neither is Buddha a revolutionary, nor Lao Tzu. Manu is revolutionary, Marx is revolutionary, Mao is revolutionary, but not Jesus, not Krishna, not Buddha. They are rebels.

A revolution is a planning. A revolution thinks of the future; a rebellion is herenow. Revolution is utopian—a dream, somewhere in the future, the golden age, the utopia, the paradise. Rebellion is to live it here and now. To be rebellious means to be transformed totally.

In revolution, and in the ideology of revolution, you try to change the others, you try to change the scene. In rebellion, you change yourself and the scene changes by itself, of its own accord, because your vision is different. You have different eyes to look with.

Rebellion is spontaneous. It has nothing to do with any ideology. Rebellion is non-ideological. Rebellion is like love; you don't think about it; you cannot think about it. Either you live it or you don't live it; either it is there or it is not there. Rebellion is a happening. If you are ready, you start living a totally different life: the life of authenticity, the life of innerness, the life of God, or whatsoever you would like to call it.

Jesus is a rebel, but even his followers misunderstood him—they thought he was a revolutionary; they organized. Then Christ disappeared, and Christianity was left behind. Christianity is the corpse, the corpse of Christ.

Christianity is again the same establishment against whom Jesus was rebellious. Christianity belongs to the same priests who crucified Jesus. Now the temple has moved. It is not in Jerusalem, it is in the Vatican; but it is the same temple. The money-changers have changed, but the money-changing is the same. The establishment is now owned by other people, by other names, in other names, but the establishment is the same. If Jesus comes back, and goes to the Vatican, he will again do the same thing. He was a rebel. A rebel simply lives out of his spontaneity; he has no idea what it should be. He acts out of his understanding; he responds to a situation, and something starts happening.

> *And Jesus went into the temple of God,*
> *and cast out*
> *all them that sold and bought in the temple,*
> *and overthrew*
> *the tables of the money-changers,*
> *and the seats of them that sold doves.*

Remember, I tell you, he had not gone there with this idea. He had not planned it, he was not thinking about it, otherwise he would have organized it. He would have gone there with a group organized to do this. Even his own disciples were not aware what was going to happen. I tell you, even Jesus was not aware what was going to happen. A man like Jesus lives from moment to moment. He's available. Whatsoever happens, he will respond to it.

It happened suddenly. He entered the temple and saw that the temple had been destroyed; that no more was it a house of prayer, that people were not praying, that people were not meditating, that people had completely forgotten the purpose of the temple, for what it existed, and that this temple was no more the abode of God. Now it had been captured by the priests.

And priests have always been against God. They live in the name of God, but they have always been against God. They teach prayer, but whatsoever they teach is false. They teach doctrines; they don't teach the truth, because you can teach the truth only if you live it. There is no other teaching about it.

I have heard a beautiful story about St. Francis, another Jesus. One day he said to his disciple, Leo, "Brother Leo, let us go to the town, and teach and preach to people."

They went into the town. They went up and down the streets

meeting people, smiling, talking to people—sometimes patting a boy, sometimes smiling at a woman, and sometimes saying a cheery word to a tired traveller. And it went on and on. But now it was almost getting dark and the sun was setting. Leo asked, "Master, when are we going to preach?"

And Francis said, "And what have we been doing? We have been preaching; we have been talking to people. They have observed us; they have listened to us. A few of them even looked into our eyes; a few of them have become aware what treasures we are carrying within our hearts. And there is no other teaching; there is no other preaching." Said St. Francis, "There is no use walking anywhere to preach, unless we preach as we walk."

A priest is not living what he is speaking. A priest goes on talking about and about and about. And whenever a temple is possessed by a priest it is destroyed. The great temple of God in Jerusalem was not destroyed by the enemies; it was destroyed by the priests. But it has always been so—the friends are the real enemies. Those who pretend they are the protectors, they are the ones who are destroying. And it has always been so, because rebellion has always been misunderstood as revolution.

Once Jesus is gone, his disciples start organizing—the doctrine, the dogma. Then the doctrine and the dogma become more important; then the future becomes more important. Then they become missionaries; not people who live in the here and now, not people who are spontaneous, not people who love, but people who talk about love. And if you argue against them, they are ready to fight. They are even ready to go to wars to defend the doctrine of love.

It happened that an authentic enquirer, a seeker, went to a rabbi, to a priest—the most famous of course of those days, and he said, "Please tell me the whole Torah, but in short. I will be standing on one leg, and you have to finish the whole Torah while I am standing on one leg."

The priest was annoyed, the rabbi became angry, and he told his disciples, "Throw this man outside the temple. He seems to be a sceptic. And this is insulting. He has insulted the sacred book; he has insulted our tradition."

Then the same enquirer went to a mystic, Hillel, and he said the same thing to him. And this is the difference between a priest and a mystic: Hillel said, "Perfectly true. In fact, the Torah is so short that I can repeat it a thousand and one times while you are standing on one leg. You stand." The man stood on one leg. Hillel said, "Do unto others what you would like to be done to you. This is the whole Torah. All else is just commentary."

You cannot annoy a mystic. The mystic cannot be forced by you to be angry, because he lives love. But the priest goes on talking about love. If you argue, if you are sceptical, if you are a doubter, he is angered—he can even kill you to help you. He can kill you because he has to defend the doctrine of love.

No other religion has created as many wars as Christianity, and all its preaching is about love. Nobody else has created as many wars as Islam, and the very word 'Islam' means peace. The word 'peace' creates war. The whole of Christianity is based on a single word 'love', but the ultimate result is crusades, wars, murders.

Why does it happen? Once religion becomes a dogma it is bound to happen. Once rebellion turns into a revolution, into an organized thing, it is bound to happen. Rebellion is individual, pure, virgin; it comes out of the heart; it is not some doctrine.

A man came to me once and he said, "I wish I had your creed. Then I would live a life like you." He repeated it: "I wish I had your creed; then I would live a life like yours."

I told the man, "You please start living the life like me. Soon you will have the creed."

The vice versa is not true—you cannot have the creed first,

and then the life. Life is the primary, the basic; creed is just a
shadow.

> *And Jesus went into the temple of God,*
> *and cast out*
> *all them that sold and bought in the temple,*
> *and overthrew*
> *the tables of the money-changers,*
> *and the seats of them that sold doves.*

> *And said unto them,*
> *It is written, My house*
> *shall be called the house of prayer . . .*

Tremendously beautiful words—he says, ". . . My house."
When you are deeply centred in yourself, you are no more a
man; you become god. That is the meaning of God: a centred
consciousness. It has no other meaning. You can become a god
if you are rooted deeply within yourself, centred. If your consciousness has become a flame, without any smoke around it,
you are a god.

When Jesus said, "It is written, My house shall be called
the house of prayer," he's not really quoting any scripture, he's
creating a scripture. He says, "It is written . . ." because those
priests won't be able to understand. He quotes the scripture,
but he is not really bothering about the scripture; he is creating
it. His each word is a scripture.

> *. . . My house*
> *shall be called the house of prayer;*
> *but ye have made it a den of thieves.*

It is no more a prayer-house, it is no more a temple.

> *And when he was come into the temple,*
> *the chief priests*
> *and the elders of the people*

came unto him as he was teaching, and said,
By what authority doest thou these things?
and who gave thee this authority?

The organized religion always asks, "By what authority?" —as if the consciousness itself is not enough authority; as if some other authority is needed; as if something from the outside has to become the proof. But consciousness in itself is the authority, the only authority—there is no other authority and no other proof. But when the priest faces a mystic like Jesus, even then he is asking about scriptures—he says, "Who has given you this authority?" He's talking about the law, the legal code. He's talking the language of the establishment, "Who has given you this authority?"—as if to be prayerful needs anybody else's authority; as if to be centred one needs any licence; as if to be centred one needs any sanction from the government.

But that is what organized religion becomes. In Christianity ridiculous things have been happening. They issue orders, and they issue recognitions that somebody has become a saint. The very word 'saint' is ugly. It comes from a root term which means 'sanction'. It means the church has sanctioned that a certain person is now a saint—the recognition of the church, as if it is a Nobel prize, or a government award. The court and the legal advisers of the government have to decide, as if it is a university degree, that now you are a Ph.D. or a D. Litt. Sainthood has no need of any sanction. Sainthood is its own sanction, it is an inner authority.

Unless you speak with your inner authority, please don't speak, don't utter a word; because those words are going to be false, untrue. The true word arises out of your own being; it is born out of you as a child is born out of a mother. You have to become pregnant with God, and then the word is born. That is the only authority; no other authority is needed.

And when he was come into the temple,
the chief priests

and the elders of the people
came unto him as he was teaching, and said,
By what authority doest thou these things?

"Who has given you the authority to overthrow the tables of the money-changers? Who has given you the authority to change the rules and regulations of the temple?"

Who gave thee this authority? Jesus must have laughed. He didn't answer them because even that is irrelevant; their question is absurd.

𝓘 have heard a story about Diogenes. He was caught by thieves. And then they brought him to a slave market. He was a beautiful man; very few people have been so beautiful . . . a very strong body. And they put him on the slave-block to be sold. He stood there smiling, humming a song, unconcerned with what was happening. Then he saw a man, a young man, very rich—his clothes were very rich, but he was standing there very absent-mindedly, maybe drunk. He was standing there in the crowd, almost asleep, depressed, sad; a deep sorrow surrounded him. Diogenes said to the thieves who had caught him, and who had brought him to the slave market, "Sell me to that man. He looks as if he needs a master."

Jesus or a Diogenes, Buddha or Mahavir, they have their own authority; they are masters of their being. It is said of Buddha that a great scholar came to him and said, "Sir, whatsoever you are saying, it is not written in the Vedas."

Buddha said, "Then write it in the Vedas."

The scholar was a little puzzled. He could not believe somebody could say that—"Write it!" The man said, "Sir, not only is that the case but sometimes you contradict. Whatsoever is written in the Vedas, you say contrary things."

Buddha said, "Then amend the Vedas. Because when I am

here, when the Veda is alive here, then the dead Veda has to be corrected according to me."

A Buddha is not to follow the Vedas; the Vedas have to follow him—because they have been created by Buddhas, other centred beings. From where is their authority? If you ask Jesus, "From where is your authority?" then, because you are asking, "Has Moses given you a certificate?" you will ask from where Moses gets his authority. And if Moses can get it directly from God, then why not Jesus?

You must have heard the beautiful story when Moses encountered God. He was moving on Mount Horeb and suddenly he heard God calling him from a thorn bush. He was afraid. He started trembling and God said, "Don't be afraid. It is I. Don't be afraid. But take your shoes off, because you are walking on holy ground." He threw off his shoes. He ran towards God, who was like a burning flame, a burning fire in the thorn bush. He could not believe his eyes, because the bush was green and the fire was burning and the bush was not burned and he asked, "Who are you? This is a miracle."

And God said, "This is nothing—because I am life, I am creative force. I am not a destroyer, I am a creator. So even when my fire is there, the bush is not burning. I cannot burn; I can only heal. I cannot wound; I can only heal."

When Moses was coming back with the message God gave him, he was afraid, because his people would ask, "By what authority? From where have you brought these ten commandments? Who are you to force these ten commandments over our heads? What is your authority?"

Moses was a little more legal than Jesus. Jesus himself says, "Moses gave you the law; I give you love." Love has something in it which is always beyond law. And if your love is legal, it is not love. "Moses gave you the law. I give you love. Moses gave you the commandments, the outer morality; I give you the inner source of all morality," says Jesus.

Moses must have been a legal mind. He was. He asked,
"People will ask, 'From whom do you bring these commandments?'"

And do you know what God said? God said, "Tell them it
is from I."

Moses asked, "Who are you, what is your name? They will
ask your name."

And God said, "Tell them, I am that I am."

What does this mean, "I am that I am"? It means: "I am not
talking from the outside, I am talking from the inside. I am your
deepest am-ness. I am your deepest I. When the superficial I
disappears, you will come to know me within yourself." All
authority is from within. And they asked Jesus: *By what authority
doest thou these things? and who gave this authority to you?* Jesus
didn't answer. Many times it seems Jesus got into trouble by
not answering. But there are things which cannot be answered.
On the last day of his life, Pontius Pilate asked, "What is
truth?" and he remained silent, because silence is truth and truth
is silence. But the governor-general could not understand it.

Governor-generals are almost always stupid people, otherwise why should they be governor-generals? Politicians are
almost always mediocre people, otherwise why should they
waste their lives in politics? Much more is available, and they
waste their lives just in competition, they are just on the ego
trip.

If Jesus had said something, he may have understood, at
least he may have thought that he understood. Jesus remained
silent. He could not understand that. He must have thought,
"This man is insulting me by not answering."

The priest asked him: *By what authority doest thou these things?
Who has given you the authority?*—and Jesus remained silent
again. Because there are things which cannot be answered.

He is his own authority. And this is his message, that everybody should be his own authority. Be your authority, be an

authority unto yourself. You are not here to follow anybody; you are here to be yourself. Your life is yours; your love is yours; your innermost core of being is your authority for everything you do. And until you become an authority unto yourself you will be moving astray; you will be following this and that. You will be following shadows, and you will never be fulfilled.

Jesus didn't say anything. Rather, he told them a parable. He is one of the greatest story-tellers.

And Jesus answered and said unto them . . .

> *. . . A certain man had two sons;*
> *and he came to the first, and said,*
> *Son, go work today in my vineyard.*
>
> *He answered and said, I will not:*
> *but afterward he repented, and went.*

He said, "No," but afterward he repented and went, and in reality said, "Yes." He said no through his mind, but he said yes from his totality.

> *And he came to the second,*
> *and said likewise,*
> *And he answered and said, I go, sir:*
> *and went not.*

He said yes through his mind, and said no from his totality.

> *Whether of them twain*
> *did the will of his father?*

asked Jesus. Who did the will of his father?—the one who said, "No," but transformed his no into a yes, or the one who said, "Yes," but whose yes was impotent, and whose yes was just a way, a polite way of saying no? Who followed? Who obeyed? *Whether of them twain did the will of his father?* asked Jesus.

The priests *say unto him, The first.*

Jesus saith unto them,
Verily I say unto you,
That the publicans and the harlots
go into the kingdom of God before you

—because you have been saying yes but doing no. Your yes is just verbal, just skin-deep—it doesn't come from your heart.

Why is this the way Jesus is answering them? He has not said anything where his authority comes from, but in a way he has said everything. He says, "Because I have said yes to my God totally, from there comes my authority: because I have obeyed him, because I have surrendered myself to him."

He's not saying that on the surface, but deep down he has asserted his authority.

Who has done the will of his father—the one who says yes and never goes to do anything about it? This is what has been done by priests and scholars, by men of learning and knowledge, and by pundits.

I have heard one ancient Indian story. A sage had a parrot and the sage used to say to everybody, "Watch out for the trap. Don't sit on the trap." Of course he meant the *maya*, the illusion of the world, the trap of greed, the trap of possessiveness, the trap of anger and violence. So he used to say to his disciples, "Watch out for the trap. Don't sit on the trap."

By and by the parrot also learned it. So whenever the sage would say it, the parrot would also repeat it, even louder than the sage. And the parrot would say, "Watch out for the trap! Don't sit on the trap!" And everybody enjoyed it.

One day by mistake, the cage of the parrot was left open, and he flew out of it. Everybody had started to love the parrot, so the sage and his disciples, they all went all over the forest to search for him. When they were reaching deeper and deeper into the forest they heard the parrot saying, "Watch out for the trap. Don't sit on the trap." So they were very happy that he was there. So, following the direction of his voice, they reached there. And what did they see? They could not believe it: he was sitting on a trap. He was trapped—sitting on a trap he was continuously repeating, "Watch out for the trap. Don't sit on the trap."

That happens to people who live in the head. Whatsoever they say, their life is just the contrary. They don't live it; they go on just repeating like a parrot. They become great scholars: they know everything about God and they have not tasted even a little bit what God means. Their life has remained untouched. Their knowledge has a separate world; it is a storage in the memory. Their heart has remained as ignorant as ever. They know much, and they know not. They seem to know much, but their ignorance is tremendous.

I was reading the autobiography of a great mystic, a Chinese mystic, who used to be the librarian of the Chinese emperor. Once somebody asked him some question, and of course it was expected that the librarian should know all the answers. He was there to read and study for the king, so whenever the king wanted to know anything he could ask the librarian.

But this librarian had a bad habit of saying to almost all questions, "I don't know." So when some minister of the emperor asked some significant question which needed to be answered and the librarian said, "I don't know," the minister became annoyed. He said, "The king pays you for it; you have to know it."

The librarian said, "The king pays for my knowledge. If the king is ready to pay for my ignorance also. . . . He pays me for things I know, but if he starts paying me for things I don't know, then his treasures will not be enough. Only a few things I know. In fact, only one thing I know," he said, "and that is myself. All else I can pretend to know. I can collect information, but that will not be knowledge."

If you go on collecting information then this will happen—
you will go on saying yes in your head and you will go on
saying no in your life. You will become a dichotomy, a split
personality. Your head will be going north; your heart will be
going south, and you will be in a constant tug of war.

That's what has happened. You know everything about love,
but have you loved? You know everything about prayer, but
have you prayed? You know everything about beauty, but have
you observed beauty, have you got lost in some beautiful phenomenon? Have you become in any moment so total that the head
and heart lose their constant tug of war? Has there ever been a
moment when you were so total that you were not? If that has
not happened, then you can go on saying yes but it will not mean
much—maybe just a polite attitude.

The so-called religious people of the world are just like the
second son who said, "I go, sir"—and went not. Even an atheist
is better because he says no. At least he is true, at least he says
whatsoever he feels. He's authentic; he says, "No, I'm not going."
A man who is authentic will sooner or later become aware. He
will become remorseful about the no; he will repent.

Remember this: the world is irreligious because of so-called
religious people. It would be better if you were never taught to
be religious. It would have been better if you were not conditioned to be religious, because all conditioning can create only
a polite yes, but not a transformation, not a mutation. Better
to say no—because if you say no, and your no is true and authentic and honest, sooner or later you will have to say yes.

Why? Because nobody can live in a no. This has to be understood—one of the most fundamental things. Nobody can live
in a no. No is negative. You cannot live in negativity; you can
live only in the positive. To live in no is to live as if in death.
No is absolutely poor; it has nothing in it; it is impotence. It
is absence; it is like darkness. It is empty, hollow. To say no is
to remain a beggar; to say yes is to become an emperor.

Nobody can live in a no, but if you have said a false yes, you can think you are living, because you say that you have said yes. That false yes can deceive you. A real no is better than a false yes because a false yes becomes a mask.

For example if you don't love someone, don't say that you love. It is better to say that you don't love; better to accept in deep humbleness that you are unable to love; then there is a possibility some day or other that love will arise, because nobody can live in a state of no-love. But if you go on saying that you love and you love not, then you can waste your whole life. That polite yes, that false yes, that false love, that dishonest love, that inauthentic attitude, can become a cloudlike thing behind which you can go on hiding. But you are wasting your life. Unless you say a total yes to life you will not have lived it to the maximum. Then you will live it at the minimum.

Say yes, and that is what I call being religious. No is a first step, yes is a second step. Nobody can avoid the first step, of saying no. If you avoid it, the second step will be false because a true yes arises only from a true no.

One who has really been an atheist can become a theist. One who has denied and doubted can attain to faith and trust. One who has from the very beginning believed, will never attain to trust. His belief is a defence. He cannot gather courage to say no, so he says yes. But if you don't have the courage to say no, how can you have courage enough to say yes? Your yes will be dead.

T̶his parable is really beautiful; it carries much implication and meaning in it.

> . . . *A certain man had two sons;*
> *and he came to the first, and said,*
> *Son, go work today in my vineyard.*

He answered and said, I will not . . .
a sincere man, and sincerity always pays
. . . but afterward he repented, and went.

I tell you, even sinners—that's what Jesus is saying, even harlots
and publicans, even sinners—can reach to God, because through
their life they were saying no, but nobody can go on saying no
eternally. One day or other you become fed up with your no,
because you are living a hollow and empty life; one day or
other you divorce yourself from your no-saying, you get married
to yes-saying; you become a yea-sayer, you become religious.

One day or other you have to drop your doubt, because
doubt is a disease. And nobody can remain ill forever; nobody
would like to remain ill forever. There is a deep natural urge to
be healthy and whole; there is a deep urge to be trusting; there
is a deep urge to say yes. Have you watched? Whenever you
say yes a certain freedom immediately bursts in you; whenever
you say no you shrink. Whenever you say no you are left alone,
cut off from the world. Whenever you say yes a bridge immediately starts spreading towards existence. Say yes and you are
related to the world, to existence. Say no and you are cut off,
unrelated.

Hate is no; love is yes. Money is no; prayer is yes. People
who are doubters, sceptical, go on accumulating money because
they cannot trust life. They feel so insecure with life that they
find security in money, in something dead. People who love,
and who have loved tremendously, loved abundantly, loved
totally and said yes to life in all the ways life demands, challenges,
people who have always been ready to say yes, they don't
gather money. There is no need. Life is such a security. In its
deepest insecurity there is security.

In its deepest challenge there is love; in its deepest hardship
there is growth. Once you have said yes you are in a let-go,
you have become religious.

Whether of them twain did the will of his father? Even the priests had to say, "The first." But up till now they were not aware that the parable was about them. That is the beauty of a parable: you become aware only when the parable has penetrated your heart. That is the beauty of the parable: from the very beginning you are not defensive. You are simply listening to a story, unaware . . . and indirectly, something is penetrating your being like an arrow.

A parable is like an arrow that appears in the beginning like a flower. You allow it because you are just listening to a story. You are not worried about it; you are not defensive. You are not alert; you are relaxed.

The priests listened to the parable. Even they answered.

> *They say unto him, The first.*
> *Jesus saith unto them,*
> *Verily I say unto you,*
> *That the publicans and the harlots*
> *go into the kingdom of God before you.*

. . . *before you:* the priests, the pundits, the rabbis, the moralists, the puritans, the so-called good guys. But they are so-called; the good has not happened. It is forced, cultivated; it may be a discipline. It gives respectability, it enhances the ego.

Observe, whenever you say no you feel the ego strongly. That's why people say no so much, because each time you say no you feel you are somebody.

Sometimes I have been watching people saying no where it was not at all necessary. A small child asks the mother, "Can I go outside and play?" and immediately she says, "No." He was not demanding anything—just a little sunlight; just with the flowers a little bit, running after the butterflies. He was not asking much, and it costs nothing. The sun is available, free; the butterflies are waiting, because if nobody chases them they don't feel good; and the flowers are there—somebody should come and

smell them; they would like to share their happiness with somebody.

And the child asks, "Can I go outside?" And the mother
says, "No." And the mother has not even pondered over it, not
even for a single moment. No comes easy, as if it is always there,
ready. You just say anything and she says no. And she knows well
that the child will go out, because he will insist again and again;
two, three times he will ask, and the fourth time she will say,
"Yes, you go out. Don't bother me so much." And she knows, and
the child knows, but still the no comes. The yes doesn't seem easy.

The servant asks for his pay. You can give him it right now
but you say, "Tomorrow." No comes easy, yes seems to be
very hard. And whenever you say yes you feel as if you are
missing, as if you are helpless.

Just go to the railway station. Ask for a ticket and the booking-
clerk may be sitting doing nothing. He starts looking in the book.
He is saying, "No. Who are you?" He's trying to feel he is also
somebody. He can give it right now, but then who will say no?

Look at the policeman standing on the crossroads, no written
on his face. Look at people's faces; this is the way to judge who is
religious and who is not. If the face says no the man is irreligious,
though he may be in the temple praying. If the face says yes,
a welcoming yes, then the man is religious. He may not ever
have gone to the temple; that doesn't matter.

*Y*es has to be earned; one has to grow towards it. It's the most
beautiful phenomenon that can happen to a man, ever. But
that is possible only if you have been honest from the very
beginning. If you have been honest in saying yes, if you have
been honest in saying no, only then an honest yes can evolve
out of it—because nobody can live with a negative attitude. But
you can live with a false positive attitude, and that's how you
have been living.

I have heard a story about a Hassid mystic. His name is Rabbi Mossey. He was very poor in the eyes of others. Himself, he was an emperor, tremendously rich, infinitely rich, but his richness was of the within.

A beggar came one day as he was sitting with his disciples, and he gave him his last coin. One disciple objected. And the objection was also meaningful, because the man to whom he gave the coin was a drunkard, who would immediately go to the pub. So the disciple said two things: "First, you don't have enough to eat today, and this is your last coin. Now the whole day and the whole night you will have to starve. Second, you have given your coin to a man who is not worthy of it—he is a thief and a drunkard. What do you say about it?"

The Hassid mystic, Mossey, said, "Shall I be more particular than God who gave the coin to me? Shall I be more particular than God? If he can give to me, a worthless man, and has not asked whether I am a sinner or a drunkard, then who am I to bother whether this man is a sinner, a thief or a drunkard?"

This is the quality of a real religious man—he's not condemnatory towards others. The false religious man is always condemnatory towards others; in fact, he tries to be a moralist just in order to condemn others. He wants to be respectable and he wants to be higher than others. He always wants to look bigger than he is, and he always tries the attitude of 'holier than you'. So whomsoever he looks at he's condemning—his whole morality is just a decoration of the ego.

Remember this: if your morality is just a decoration, and your prayer and meditation just flowers to decorate around the ego so that it looks a little beautiful, then you are not religious. And Jesus is right . . .

Verily I say unto you,
That the publicans and the harlots
go into the kingdom of God before you

—because they have said no; and they will repent, and they will feel remorse, and they will not be able to live with the no. Nobody can live with the no.

Try to live with any no—anger, hatred, jealousy, possessiveness—try to live with any no. Just remain with it. Don't try to change it; don't hide it and don't suppress it, and you will see you cannot live. And when you cannot live, you drop them and you start moving towards a yes. The yes is the temple of God.

And when the chief priests and the Pharisees
had heard his parables,
they perceived that he spake of them.

But it was too late then—he had made his point clear. And he had not only made his point clear to the rabbis and the priests, he had made his point clear, even more clear, to others who were standing there.

Always remember, ordinary people have more understanding than the so-called religious people, because an ordinary man has no investment in religion. The priest has an investment in religion. He's on guard always. And people like Jesus can be dangerous. If they are heard and their message spreads, then the priest will disappear. Temples will be there, but the priests will disappear. Religion will be there, but the exploitation that goes on in the name of religion will disappear.

The priest is always afraid of the prophet; the priest is always afraid of the mystic; the priest is always afraid of the really religious, the authentically religious person.

But when they sought to lay hands on him,
they feared the multitude,
because they took him for a prophet.

Now not only have they understood the parable, but the people who were listening there, they have also understood it. It was so clear. Now it is difficult to lay hands on Jesus. They had tried in every way to stop Jesus. They had wanted to throw him into prison; they had wanted to kill him. They did whatsoever they could, but they were always afraid of the multitude, of the crowd, of the ordinary people—for these are more sensitive; they can see things more clearly; their eyes are not so clouded as the eyes of pundits and scholars, the knowers.

They had to wait for the right moment. They crucified him in the end, but they had to wait for the right moment. And the right moment came, when they could persuade the political power that this man was not talking religion, that this man was not a rebel—this man was a revolutionary. They persuaded the political powers: "This man is not talking about the kingdom of God—that is just a strategy. This man is talking about this kingdom on the earth. This man is not trying to lead people towards God; this man is trying to possess power; the kingdom of this earth, for himself. He is against the government."

When they could persuade the government, only then. . . . And remember, there is always a conspiracy between the priests and the political leaders. They have always been in conspiracy; they help each other. Whenever the politician needs his position sanctified by religion, the priest comes to help. He says, "The king is no ordinary human being. He is an incarnation of God." He says, "He is made king by God himself. His authority is not in himself but in God; he's just a representative of God on earth."

That's how the priests help the king, the political power, and give him an aura of religion and divineness; that's how kings have existed up to now.

And so the priest is in difficulty from the mystics, and both the king and the priest are in difficulty from the mystics, because the mystic is a rebel. A mystic is a rebellion. His very being is so free that he would like to liberate everybody else. His message is liberation, freedom—total, absolute freedom. The king is afraid; the priests help. The priest is afraid; the king helps.

The priests and the political power both joined together to

kill this innocent man who had no power at all; or, his power
was not of this world—his power was that of a meek and humble
man; his power was that of a realized man. The power is not
violent. His power is that of love, what Lao Tzu calls 'the man
of tao'. He is powerful, because he is powerless. He is supremely
high, because he lives at the lowest point. He's at the peak,
because he lives in the darkest valley. He's great, because he
does not claim greatness. The power of the meek, the power of
the humble, the power of the egoless, the power of one who is
not . . . then the power of God enters. Then he becomes the
vehicle for the whole.

The last thing: be alert, because in each of you these three
possibilities are all hidden. You can be a priest if you say a
false yes and you can also be a scholar accumulating much
knowledge and information. The second: if you say no, but
cling to it and don't go ahead, if you make your abode in no,
then you become an atheist, a doubter. The priest misses because
of the false yes and you will miss because of a true no. But if
these are the only alternatives, I would like you to say the no,
because at least it is true and honest; and through honesty there
is some possibility. Be an atheist, but don't be a false religious
man.

Then there is a third possibility: that you say an authentic
no but don't cling to it; you don't make it your abode. Good,
if you rest for a night, but then in the morning start moving—
because no will be a suicide. Don't commit suicide with no.
Don't be a hypocrite with a false yes and don't be suicidal with
a true no.

The third is the right direction. Say an authentic no and go
on moving. That is not the end—just the beginning, the first
step. And the yes has to be born in you. If you allow it, it will
be born. If you go on moving, observing, living, experiencing,

and not falsifying things, looking at things as they are, sooner or later the yes is born; you become pregnant with yes. Then you are the temple. Then there is no need to go to any other temple. Then God descends in you. In fact, no man has ever found God. Whenever man is ready, God finds him.

6 *A man who is enlightened has no masks, has no character,*
has no rules to follow.

I myself am a question. I know not who I am.
What to do? Where to go?

REMAIN WITH THE QUESTION. Don't do anything, and don't
go anywhere; and don't start believing in any answer.
Remain with the question. That is one of the most difficult
things to do—to remain with a question, and not to seek the
answer; because the mind is very cunning, it can supply a false
answer. It can console you; it can give you something to cling to;
and then the question is not answered but suppressed. Then you go
on believing in the answer, and the question remains deep down in
your unconsciousness like a wound. The healing has not happened.

If you remain with the question, I'm not saying that you will
receive the answer. Nobody has ever received any answer. If you
remain with the question, by and by the question disappears. Not
that the answer is received; there is no answer. There cannot be,
because life is a mystery. If there is any answer, then life will not
be a mystery.

It has no answer to it, it cannot be solved. It is not a puzzle, it is a mystery. And that is the difference between a puzzle and a mystery. A puzzle can be solved, howsoever difficult it is to solve. A mystery cannot be solved—not that it is difficult. It is very simple, but its nature is such that it cannot be solved.

Remain with the question—alert, aware, not seeking, not trying to find an answer. Very arduous it is, but if you can do that . . . it can be done. I have done it. And all those who have dissolved their questions have done it. The very awareness, the fire of awareness, burns the question. The sun of awareness melts the question; it disappears, it evaporates. One day, suddenly, you find you are there, and the question is not there. Not that the question is replaced by an answer. There is none. But the question has simply disappeared. You are there and without a question. That is the answer.

You, without a question, is the answer. Not that you will be able to say who you are—you will laugh at the very question. The question has become absurd. In the first place, the very asking was wrong. But right now you cannot understand that; you have to ask. You have to ask very intensely. Ask the question, but don't ask for the answer.

That is the difference between theology and religion. Theology gives you the answer; religion gives you awareness. Theology supplies you answers—ready-made, manufactured, polished, perfect. Religion doesn't give you any answer; it simply helps you to penetrate deep into the question. The deeper you go into the question, the more you find it is melting, it is disappearing. And when the question has disappeared, a tremendous energy is released within you. You *are* there, with no question.

And when there is no question, of course, there is no mind. Mind is the questioner. When there is no questioning, the mind has also disappeared—pure consciousness—just the sky without any clouds, the flame without any smoke.

That's what God is. That's what a Buddha is; that's what a

Christ is. Remember, I repeat it again and again, Buddha has not found the answer; that's why Buddha never answers. You ask him, "God exists?" He will avoid, he will not answer. You ask him, "What happens when a Buddha dies?" He will avoid, he will start talking about other things. He will not answer.

He is not a metaphysician. He is not a philosopher. He has come to face the question, and the question has disappeared. The question disappears as darkness disappears when you kindle a light, when you bring a lamp. Bring more awareness to the question.

You ask me: *Bhagwan, I myself am a question.* Beautiful—that's how it should be—reduce all questions to the basic question and that is: Who am I? Don't go on moving on the periphery, like —"Who made the world? Why did he make the world?"—all nonsense questions. Come to the basic question, the most fundamental question: Who am I?

Who? Let your consciousness penetrate into it, like a deep arrow going deeper and deeper and deeper. And don't be in a hurry to find the answer—because the mind is cunning. If you are in a hurry, impatient, the mind can supply you with it; the mind can quote scriptures; it is the devil. It can say, "Yes, you are god, you are *brahma*, you are pure consciousness, *satchitananda*, you are the ultimate truth, the eternal soul, the deathless being." Those answers can destroy your very search.

A seeker has to be aware of ready-made answers. They are available; from every side they are being supplied to you. In fact, your mind has already been conditioned: the answers have been given to you before you had even asked the question.

A small child—he has not asked who God is, and he is being supplied with the answer; he is being conditioned. He has not asked—the question is still not there, and the answer is being given. Many people go on believing in these answers, and they never ask the question themselves.

If you have not asked the question, whatsoever you know is

just rubbish. Throw it on the rubbish heap, all your knowledge
—because there is no knowledge; there is only knowing. There
is no answer, only a state of consciousness where the questioning
disappears; only a clarity, a clarity of vision and perception, a
clarity of eyes, you can see through and through; not that you
find an answer somewhere. Existence is so vast, so mysterious.

And it is good that it is so. Just think of the misfortune if you
could have found the answer. Then life would not be worth
living; then it would not have any meaning. Because you cannot
find the answer, the life goes on having infinite meaning. God is
not the answer. God is the state of being where the question has
disappeared. God is the state of no-mind.

Remain with the question. I am here to help you to remain
with the question. I am not going to give you any answer;
you already have too many. I am not going to burden you any
more. I am to teach you how to unlearn the answers that you
have learned, so that the question becomes crystal pure; so the
question becomes authentic and yours; so the question arises
from your innermost being.

And remain with it. Don't go here and there; don't be in a
hurry. Be patient. Let this question become your constant com-
panion. This is the only discipline I teach you: the discipline of
questioning, and without being in any hurry for the answer.

And it is beautiful to remain with the question because
answers corrupt. They destroy your innocence; they destroy your
pure ignorance. They fill your mind with words, theories,
dogmas; then you are no more a virgin. They corrupt you. The
question is pure; it does not corrupt you. In fact, it intensifies
your purity; it makes you more and more clear.

Become aware of the question. Not that you have to continuously ask, "Who am I?" Not that you have to verbalize it.
Let the question be there without any verbalization. Let it be like

your breathing; let it be like your being. Let it be there, silent, but continuously, as if you are pregnant with it. One day, if you have lived enough with the question, it starts disappearing. It evaporates, just as when the morning comes and the sun rises, and the dewdrops start disappearing. When the consciousness has become a fire, an intense light, the question starts disappearing.

And when the question has disappeared, you cannot say who you are, but you know. It is not a knowledge; it is a knowing. You cannot answer, but you know. You can dance it; you cannot answer it. You can smile it; you cannot answer it. You will live it, but you cannot answer it.

My anger has lessened, my sexual desire is not my master, my mind is more still, and still I know I am not surrendered to you. What will it take—a thunderbolt?

The first thing to be understood: you cannot surrender; it is not something you can do. If *you* are there, then how is the surrender possible? If the doer is there, then how can the surrender happen? It is not an act. When *you* are not there, then the surrender *is*. So you cannot surrender—one thing is absolutely certain. *You* cannot surrender, because *you* is the barrier. And this is what you have been trying, trying to surrender. It is like trying to go to sleep: try hard, and then failure is absolute. Sleep comes when you are not there and the effort has ceased. When you are trying no more to go to sleep—you have completely forgotten about it, because any activity is against sleep—if you are trying to go to sleep. . . . That's what so many people who suffer from sleeplessness, insomnia, are doing all over the world. They try: they do many tricks; they count sheep, they do transcendental meditation, they do *mantras*, and a thousand and one things they do to get to sleep, because they don't know that the *doer* is the barrier. Sleep comes when you are not.

Sometimes those *mantras* may appear to help, because by doing a *mantra*, you by and by get fed up with it; you are bored. That is the whole mechanism of a *mantra*, that it bores you. You become so bored that the *mantra* drops; and in your boredom the very effort to get to sleep also drops. Suddenly the sleep is there. Sleep comes when you are not. The truth comes when you are not. The God comes when you are not. Surrender is not something that you can do. You can only be receptive for it to happen; it is a happening.

You ask: *My anger has lessened*—good! *My sexual desire is not my master*—very good! *My mind is more still*—beautiful! The situation is building itself. Now don't be in a hurry to surrender. Everything happens only in its own time. Ripeness is all; just don't be in a hurry; the fruit is ripening every day. The moment is coming closer and closer when suddenly, without any previous notice, the fruit falls from the tree.

Just like that, surrender happens. You will not be notified, remember. There is nobody going to say to you, "Now, surrender is going to happen!" There is not going to be any announcement of it. In fact when it happens, in that moment, you are surprised, taken unawares; you were not expecting it.

Remember this, while you are expecting it, it is not going to happen, because when you are expecting, you are there. It happens only when you are not expecting at all; in fact, you have forgotten about it. Suddenly it is there.

Have you observed?—sometimes it happens you have forgotten the name of someone. And you know that you know. And you say, "It is just on the tip of my tongue." And still, you cannot recall it. Try hard. The more you try, the more it will be frustrating. The more you try hard, the more you will be in a weird situation. You know it—it is right on the tip of the tongue—and it is not coming. One feels at a loss; one cannot think what is happening.

Then you try, and try, and try, and it doesn't come. You are fed up with the whole effort. You go out of the house; you start digging in the garden, and suddenly it is there. It bubbles up to the surface.

What happened? Try to understand the mechanism. It was there, but the very effort made you tense. And a tense mind is a narrow mind, the tenser the narrower. The mind became so narrow and so tense, so one-pointed that the name could not pass through it. Your mind became like a needle's eye, and the camel could not pass through it. You knew it was there, but the very effort narrowed you, because effort means concentration.

Remember, I don't teach concentration; I teach meditation. And the difference is this: concentration is a narrowing of the mind. And I tell you, that even a camel can pass through the eye of a needle, but one who is concentrating cannot pass through the gates of God—because the mind becomes narrower and narrower. That is the whole meaning of concentration. Meditation is not concentration. Meditation is simple awareness—widening of the mind, widening of consciousness—expansion, not narrowing.

Meditation is all-inclusive. You listen to me . . . if you are listening to me, and at the same time the crowing of the crows is not reaching your consciousness, it is concentration. Then you may remember what I am saying, but you will never understand —because a narrow mind cannot understand much. But while I'm speaking and the crow is crowing and the birds are singing —and you are not narrowed; you are flowing in all directions, aware of all—in this moment, your consciousness is open to every possibility that is happening. Then I am talking and the crow is crowing and there is no conflict, because the conflict arises only when you are concentrating.

There is no conflict. In the same moment, simultaneously, all is happening. Each moment is multi-dimensional. If you are

simply aware, you listen to me and you listen to the crow also.
And you are not disturbed. Only people who concentrate are
disturbed and distracted. A man who meditates is never distracted,
because nothing can distract him. He's not narrowing his mind;
he's not excluding anything—he's all-including. He's simply here
and now. And whatsoever happens—if God feels like crowing
through the crow—perfectly good. And if he thinks of singing
a song through a bird—perfectly beautiful. Then everything is
accepted; then the total is allowed.

When you are trying to remember a name or a word, the
more you try, the less possibility there is of succeeding—because
the mind is becoming narrower and narrower and narrower.
Then you drop the whole effort; you relax in your chair and start
smoking—and suddenly it is there. The mind is narrow no more;
the tension is gone—effort is no more there; you have become
effortless. Then you have become meditative.

Meditation is effortless awareness; concentration is a narrowing of the mind with much effort. I teach meditation; I teach
expansion of consciousness, an ability to flow in all directions
simultaneously.

Open up all the doors of your being. Why be narrow? Let the
sky enter from all the doors; let the light come from all the
windows; let the breeze blow from all the directions. Why be
narrow? Accept—total, meditative. Then one day, suddenly,
you are surprised: surrender has happened. You were not trying
to do it, and it has happened. It has always been so. You cannot
surrender. One day when you are in a relaxed mood. . . .

Remember, when you are in a relaxed mood, you are not.
You are, only when you are in a tense mood. When you are
relaxed you are part of the whole; you are not. Then boundaries
are blurred; then the whole and the part are no more separate.
They meet, they merge . . . surrender happens.

So, good that anger is lessened; sexual desire is no more the master; the mind is getting still. Now please, don't make any effort to surrender. Otherwise the mind will again become tense, and the stillness will be lost. And again you will become angry —because when you cannot surrender, you become angry, angry against yourself. And then sooner or later you will find the sex has again become the master.

When the mind is angry—it doesn't matter, angry against others or against yourself, it doesn't matter—when the mind is angry and when the mind is tense, sex becomes the master, because then sex is the only release. Then you are so much tense that you have to throw some energy out some way. Then sex becomes the outlet.

It is a safety valve, a natural safety valve. The nature has given you an opening: if you cannot cope with your energy and you cannot remain relaxed, then the energy goes on accumulating, and there comes a point when it has to be released; otherwise you will go mad. Mad people all over the world are somehow or other mad, because they suppressed their sex energy. Either transform it, or don't suppress it.

Sex becomes the master because you are so tense. You need it; you need its help. When you are relaxed, sex disappears. The more you are relaxed, the more sex disappears. If you are totally relaxed, sex disappears completely; and the energy that was involved in sex becomes love, becomes compassion, becomes awareness, becomes freedom.

And the last thing: *What will it take—a thunderbolt?* You go on thinking about ego as if it is a very very big and strong thing. It is not. It is just a water bubble, a soap bubble. It does not need a thunderbolt; just a small prick and it is gone—and the bigger it is, the weaker; the stronger it is, the weaker.

This paradox has to be understood. It's just as if you make a soap bubble, and go on making it bigger and bigger and bigger. The bigger the bubble, the more the emptiness in it; the bigger the bubble, the weaker—sooner or later it is going to explode. If it was small, it was stronger.

That's why I say that the ego has to be strengthened, so that it becomes weak and bursts. The bigger the balloon, the more emptiness it carries. Just a prick. . . . That's why it was so easy for a Buddha to attain to truth, because he was the son of an emperor. A big balloon he must have carried within, a big ego—he was no ordinary man. It must have been more difficult for Jesus than it was for Buddha. He was just a son of a carpenter, a poor man's son. It must have been very difficult for him to drop it. For Buddha it was simple; in fact it dropped of its own accord, it was so big, so empty.

So don't wait for a thunderbolt. Just a small breeze. . . . Your ego is nothing but a dewdrop on a grass leaf. A small breeze and it slips and is gone. It happens very easily. But I am saying: it happens. You cannot do. If you do, then even thunderbolts won't help. It happens. You just go on becoming more and more still, silent, peaceful, loving; and one day, when the time has come, when the right moment has arrived, when the ego is ripe, it slips. And when it slips, it is beautiful, because it doesn't leave a trace behind.

If you drop it, it never drops. First, you were thinking you were somebody; then you start thinking you are nobody. First, it was hiding behind 'somebodiness'; now it will hide behind 'nobodiness'. First, you were thinking you were something extraordinary, a rare gem, a kohinoor; now you will think, "I am the most humble man in the world"—but the *most* humble —remember. "There is nobody who is more humble than me— I am the humblest." Now it is hiding in your humbleness. The wound has not disappeared; only the label has changed. You are the same; you have moved from one extreme to another, but nothing is transformed.

A man whose ego has disappeared is not humble at all. Because how can you be humble without an ego? A man whose ego has disappeared—his ego has disappeared, that's all; and with the ego, all humbleness also—because humbleness is a quality of the ego; it is a function of the ego. A man who is egoless is not humble at all. He is neither humble nor arrogant; he simply *is*.

What constitutes the behaviour of an enlightened man?

An enlightened man is an emptiness. What constitutes an emptiness? It has no 'constitutes' in it; hence it is empty. A man who is enlightened has no character.

Let me repeat it: an enlightened man has no character at all. He lives from moment to moment. He has no character to follow; he has no structure around him. A character is a structure, a character is an armour. An enlightened man has no character. Let me say he is characterless.

But try to understand me—because he has no structured consciousness. He *has* consciousness but the structure has been dropped. He's neither Hindu nor Mohammedan nor Christian. He is neither good nor bad, neither moral nor immoral, neither this nor that. He simply is. All duality has disappeared. You cannot evaluate him; you cannot categorize him; you cannot put him into any pigeon-holes of your logic. He exists like an emptiness—nothingness he is. And out of that nothing, every moment the miracle—that he goes on functioning without any armour around him, without any structure. He goes on flowing.

It is difficult for you to understand, because you cannot think how you would function without a structure. If you don't have any morality conditioned on you, how will you behave morally? —it seems difficult for you. It is just like saying to a blind man that we walk without groping. The blind man says, "I cannot believe you. How can one walk without groping? Groping is a must." The blind man has his stick; he goes on groping with his stick—"Where is the door?"—and if you say that we don't carry any sticks, he will laugh: "You must have gone mad, or you must be joking." And he will say to you, "Don't be funny. Don't try to be funny. Because if you don't grope with a stick, how can you walk?"

Our character is like the blind man's staff. We grope in darkness; we somehow manage to be good; we somehow manage to be moral. And inside, the immorality goes on and on, ready to explode any moment—a great turmoil within. And we go on managing somehow on the surface. That's what we call character.

A man who is enlightened—who has come to know who he is, who has faced himself—has no masks, has no character, has no rules to follow. There is no need, because each moment his consciousness is there, and out of his consciousness arises his act.

You act out of your conscience; he acts out of his consciousness. Conscience is given by the society; consciousness is your nature. You act 'good', because you have been told to act 'good'. Not that you are good. You *act* 'good' because you know it pays to be good; you know honesty is the best policy. Just see: it is policy, it is politics. It is cunningness, because it pays. And if dishonesty pays—if dishonesty is the best policy—then you move to dishonesty.

That's how the hypocrite is born. He goes on pretending to be honest, and he goes on doing whatsoever pays. Sometimes honesty pays—then he is honest; sometimes dishonesty pays— more often dishonesty pays—then he goes on being dishonest. Whatsoever pays, whatsoever fulfils your greed. . . .

A man who is enlightened lives out of his consciousness. He has no conscience. He has thrown out all that structure, that conditioned mind. Now he lives out of his purity, innocence.

His act is here and now; your act is mind-manipulated. You do something, but either it comes from the past, because you have been conditioned to do it that way, or it comes from the future, because you have been told about awards in heaven and somewhere in the future. Either it comes out of fear, or it comes out of greed—it never comes out of your consciousness. The enlightened man lives out of his consciousness.

Let me say it in a different way: you react, he acts. Somebody insults you: immediately you react. There is no time gap. You become angry, you retaliate. If you insult a Buddha, there is a time gap. He does not react. He looks at you; he watches you; he observes you: "Why are you behaving in this way?" And out of that observation he responds. It is not a reaction; it is not a push-button thing. Somebody insults you; he has pushed a button. You react; you go mad. You cannot push any button in a Buddha; he has no buttons. That's what I mean: he has no character around him. You cannot push any button. He has dropped the whole mechanism. You can be angry; you can insult him; but you cannot decide his reaction, because he has none.

Once it happened: A few people insulted him very badly . . . abused him. He listened, listened very silently—you cannot find a greater listener than Buddha. Those people started feeling a little awkward, because they were waiting for him to react; and he was listening so silently, so meditatively, as if they were reciting the Vedas; and they were just abusing him. They started feeling awkward, because the expected reaction was not coming.

One of them asked, "Are you listening or not to what we are saying? Your face has not changed even a little bit. You don't seem to be angry."

Buddha said, "Because I am listening to you, I feel much compassion. Poor fellows—why are you in such a rage, and why are you in such an anger? Why are you poisoning your systems?" Buddha is thinking about them.

They said, "Forget about us. We have not come to ask for any advice. What about you?"

Buddha said, "If you had come ten years before, then I would have reacted. You came a little late. Now you can insult me, but it never reaches me, because I never accept it. And unless I accept it—unless at my end I receive it—you cannot give me anything. You can give; but I don't take it."

Buddha told them a parable. He said, "Just in the other village people had come with many sweets, but I told them that I didn't need sweets—'Please take them back.' I ask you, what should they have done about those sweets?"

Those people gathered there said, "They must have distributed them in the town."

Buddha laughed and said, "Now what will you do? You have brought abuses, insults, anger, hatred, and I say to you, 'I don't take them.' Now you will have to take them back and distribute them in the village. I feel sorry for you."

This is action. And remember, reaction binds; action is freedom, action has no bondage. If you act, you are free; if you react, you are in the bondage to it. Act means total—out of your total consciousness a response comes—not out of conscience, not out of concepts, not out of the mind, but out of your being, the innermost being, which is beyond you. Your nature is beyond you—it comes from there.

An enlightened man is a miracle every moment. He remains in absolute silence, and acts out of that silence, responds out of that silence. He has no ideas about good and bad, but whatsoever happens through him is good. Whatsoever happens through him is love, whatsoever happens through him is compassion, because it is not possible otherwise. Not that he decides, "I should love you." He has no 'shoulds', no ideals. Not that he decides, "I should not be bad; I should not sin"—he has no ideas about 'bad' or 'sin'.

Out of awareness is virtue born. Whatsoever comes out of awareness is virtue, and whatsoever comes out of your sleep is sin. If you ask my definition of sin, I will say, "An unconscious act, which is a reaction, is sin. A conscious act which is not a reaction—which is a response—is virtue."

The fourth and the fifth question . . . but before I take them, I will tell you a parable; before I even read the questions to you, I will tell you the parable.

*I*t happened once: There was a small village of artists in Tibet. For centuries they had developed one art. The art was of twisting wires, metals, into beautiful forms: of man, animals, birds, gods, angels. And they had become tremendously efficient in it. All over Tibet they were known as 'the expert twisters'. And by and by they also became very rich, because their goods were sold all over the country. Their goods had even started to be sold in India and China, and beyond the borders.

The village became very very rich and affluent. And as it happens always: whenever a society, a village, a family, a man, becomes very affluent, the awareness dawns that this whole success has been a failure. Because riches are there, but the poverty is not destroyed by them. In fact, only a rich man knows how poor he is. A poor man is never so poor; he cannot compare, he has nothing to compare his poverty against. And a poor man is never hopeless; he goes on hoping. Some day or other, he will attain to happiness, he will attain to riches and success. But a rich man—a man who has succeeded—fails utterly, because suddenly he becomes hopeless; now there is no hope. Whatsoever could be attained, he has attained—and nothing has been attained. For the first time, the inner poverty erupts into consciousness.

In that village it happened—as it is happening in America today—in that village it happened: people had become affluent, very rich. Their goods were sold all over Asia. And by and by they became aware that this whole life seemed to be pointless . . . just continuously twisting wires, metals, and bringing more and more money into the homes. But for what? There seemed to be no meaning in it.

So they decided to invite a sage who used to live in the hills, to tell them the secret of life. Because all that this world could give, they had, but everything seemed to be pointless.

The sage came. Before he even uttered a single sentence, he knew what was going to happen. But still he spoke. He said, "Unless you die, you will not attain to the meaning you are asking for. Unless you lose yourself, you will not gain yourself." He talked about surrender, egolessness.

One man stood up and he said, "Wait. This is impossible. I am; how can I surrender my am-ness? Who will surrender it? It is impossible. You are talking nonsense."

Another man said, "If I lose myself, what is the guarantee that I will gain my self about which you are talking?"

Another said, "You are just talking absurdities. We have asked you to come to teach us life, and you are teaching death. What you are saying to us means: should we commit suicide?"

The sage laughed and he said, "I knew beforehand what was going to happen. I know your disease. For centuries, and for generations and generations, you have been twisting wires and metals; you have become expert twisters. So I knew it beforehand: whatsoever I would say, you would immediately twist it."

It seems that from that village, one man has come here.

Now I will read the two questions. He has asked many, but there is no need of them—two will give you the vision of how things can be twisted.

First question:

> *You have given me your love. Now I want you to*
> *hate me. Can you?*

My love is not the opposite of hate; it is the absence of hate. So I cannot hate you. Your love is just the opposite of hate, not the absence of hate; so in fact, when you say to somebody, "I love you," at the same time hate is present in you. The very moment you say to somebody, "I love you," go and search within yourself, and you will find that you also hate the same person. That is what is going on between each and every lover. They fight, they love, they hate. They are continuously shifting from love to hate, from hate to love.

My love is not the opposite of hate. So please don't challenge me: that I cannot do. There comes my limitation. That's why I say God cannot be omnipotent, because he cannot hate; it is impossible.

But what is the point?—I am here to teach you love, and you are challenging me to hate you. Twisters! And for what have you come here? And what is the point of such stupid questions? But you must be thinking in your mind that you are asking great questions.

Second question:

> *Do you think that you will be unable to work upon me*
> *if I do not take your sannyas?*

Have you come to find your capacities or have you come to find my capacities? Are *you* your problem, or am I your problem? Leave me to myself; you at least solve yourself. And you don't know what you are asking. What is sannyas? It is just a gesture, a gesture that you are receptive towards me, a gesture that you welcome me in your heart, a gesture that if I come you will not reject me, a gesture that you are ready to come with me, to walk with me, to follow me—a gesture, I say.

And you ask me, "Do you think that you will be unable to work upon me if I do not take your sannyas?" You are asking the sunlight, "Will you be able to come into my house if I don't open my doors?" If you don't open your doors, how can the sunlight come in?

To be a sannyasin is just to open your doors for me. I cannot force my way into you; that would be violence, that wouldn't be love. I cannot force any change in you. That would be violence; and through violence how can God be born? How can you be reborn out of violence?

The sun will stand outside the door. It will not even knock, because you may be fast asleep and dreaming beautiful dreams; and who knows, you may be disturbed, and who am I to disturb you? If you have decided to be fast asleep and dreaming, who am I to change your decision?

I am not violent; I am not a mahatma. You have become accustomed to know mahatmas. Mahatmas are violent people who are chasing you, chasing after you. Anyhow they have to change you—obsessed with *your* change. But why should I be obsessed with your change? It is for you to decide; it is up to you to make it or not make it.

I am like a river flowing by. If you feel thirsty, come. You challenge the river, "If I don't bend, and if I don't make a cup out of my hands, are you capable of quenching my thirst?" But why should I? Thirst is yours. Who am I to quench it? If you have decided to remain thirsty, it is up to you—I bless your thirst. Remain thirsty. If you have decided to remain a desert, who am I to change you, and why? And how is it possible if you have decided to remain a desert, to make a garden out of you? Impossible . . . because you are alive, you are energy, cosmic energy. You will resist; you will fight; and whatsoever I will do, you will destroy.

Sannyas is just a gesture—a gesture from your side, a signal that you are ready. Just a signal from your heart that you are welcoming, that you will receive me. I can make love to you, but I cannot rape you. And you are asking for rape.

Whatsoever I say, you will twist it. I am not saying these things for the person who has asked the question. He comes from that village; he will twist. I am saying these things for those who don't come from that village. They may understand.

This morning in the dancing meditation I found myself
crying heart-rent tears of happiness. What is this
strange paradox?

Life is a paradox; paradox is its nature. It is not strange. But you are so much addicted to logic that whenever life reveals itself to you, it looks strange. Logic has been continuously taught to you—that contradictory things cannot exist together. Logic has been teaching you that either it is day or it is night; either it is life or it is death; either it is happiness or it is un-happiness. The whole mechanism of logic is of 'either-or'.

And life is both together. Life is all together. Whenever you reach to the deepest sadness, suddenly you will see it is turning into happiness. Or, you reach to the deepest happiness and you will see that it is turning into sadness. At the centre they meet; only on the periphery are they separate.

It is just as if you make a circle, and from the centre you can draw many lines towards the periphery. On the periphery, the circumference, the lines are very far away. Move towards the centre and by and by they come closer and closer, and exactly on the centre they become one point.

All paradoxes meet within you; all paradoxes meet in exis-

tence. Only on the periphery of the mind are they separate.
Deep in you, life and death are both one. Deep in you, happiness and unhappiness are both one. Deep in you, God and the
devil are both you. Deep in you, this world and the other are
both one, this shore and the other shore are both one.

But whenever you come for the first time to that point of
realization, it looks strange, unfamiliar. But I tell you, if you are
really happy, tears will come. It is impossible if the happiness
has gone really deep—it cannot be without tears. Of course, the
quality of those tears is absolutely different. It is not of sadness;
it is of overflow.

And remember, if you have not known sadness together with
happiness you have not known anything yet. Then your happiness is superficial; your sadness is also superficial. Then you have
been living on the surface; then you have known only the waves;
you have not known the depth of the ocean that you are.

Life is contradictory, paradoxical. It has to be so, because
only then can it be so rich. If your happiness cannot cry and
weep, it will be shallow, it cannot be rich. And if your tears
cannot laugh, and if your sadness cannot dance, then it is superficial. In the depth, the sadness becomes a song—a tremendous
beauty of silence surrounds you, and a song is born out of the
depth.

If you look into it, you will find you are not sad. The sadness
is there, the happiness is there, and you are neither. This is the
innermost triangle of existence; this is the point of transcendence
where opposites meet. You immediately transcend. You become
the third, immediately. When you see happiness and sadness
meeting, suddenly you are separate from both; all identity is
broken. Then you know you are a witness. Now it is for you to
be identified—either, if you want, you can be identified with
sadness or you can be identified with happiness. When you are
identified with happiness, sadness is suppressed; when you are
identified with sadness, happiness is suppressed—but both are

two aspects of the same coin; and you are the master. The coin is in your hand; you are not the coin at all.

When opposites meet, you transcend. So don't be worried about the strange experience. Allow it! Because if you become worried, you will stop allowing it—because you will start feeling it is something like madness. You have known only mad people who can both smile and cry together. The East knows better. In the West, if you cry and laugh together, immediately you will be taken to the psychiatrist. Something has gone wrong. You are contradictory. You are mad. In the East we know better.

Madmen and mystics have something in common: the mystic has transcended beyond the duality, and the madman has fallen below it; but they are both out of the duality; they have a similarity. A mystic can laugh and weep, and sometimes there have been rare mystics: for example, Gurdjieff. He could weep from one eye and laugh from another. He could deceive people —one sitting on the left side, the other on the right. And when they would both go out they would both report different things about him. And they would both start quarrelling and saying, "You are wrong. That man was very sad; I have even seen a tear drop from his eye."

And the other would contradict. He would say, "You must have gone mad, because I have seen his eyes so sparkling with happiness." Only later on, people became aware that he was playing games.

A mystic has transcended. He has become the master through his transcendence. A madman has fallen below. But both have one thing in common—the madman has something of the mystic, and the mystic has something of the madman. So sometimes in the West, mystics have been forced to live in madhouses; and sometimes in the East, madmen have been worshipped as mystics.

The boundaries are a little blurred. But don't be afraid. The fear comes because you see something like madness inside; you become afraid. Don't be afraid—otherwise what am I here for? Don't be afraid. Whenever something like this happens and you get scared, remember me, and go on and on. Never escape from the innermost core; because if you once escape from it, that will become a block. Then again and again you will go to the same point, and the fear will grip you and you will fall back.

Don't create such blocks. Go on and on. That is the meaning of sannyas: so you can trust me when the need arises. When you feel too much alone, and when you feel paradoxical things happening in you—where life looks like death and you are scared—you can lean on my shoulder, you can remember me. You can gather courage and you can go on. Once you go on, you know that it was nothing. That phase has passed; but that you will know only when you have gone on and on and on.

Spiritual growth has many hazards, many danger points. If you escape from those points once, you become afraid forever. So trust me, and trust yourself, and go on. There is nothing to fear, because the closer you are coming to yourself, the closer you are coming to real sanity. The further away you are from your centre, the further away you are from sanity. The world may call you sane, but you know that you are not.

Bhagwan, here with you is the deepest, most growing place for me to be and I dislike much of what I see here —dead Rajneeshianity rising like an ikon, licentiousness not freedom emerging, arrogance and aggressiveness the rule, humility and caring the exception. Opening to the awareness that these are my qualities, projected, returns me to a deep appreciation in being here. Thank you.

This is from Amitabh. I can only say, "Thank you, Amitabh." If you can understand that this is your own mind projecting things, nothing need be said. You have understood the right thing. Always remember, the whole world acts like a screen, and you go on projecting yourself. Whatsoever you say about others, says more about you. It does not say anything about others; because how can you know others?—you don't even know yourself.

If this awareness has come to you, that this is your own projection—beautiful. Keep it; hold it fast so it does not slip away. And not only about this ashram: about the whole world. Always remember, that you go on seeing your own face. The world acts like a mirror.

And that should never be your worry—how the world is—because nothing can be done about that. All that can be done has to be done by you, with you, upon yourself. Once you change, your projections will disappear. Once *you* change, the world will remain the same, but it will not be the same at all.

Because you are your world. It comes out of you, and spreads outwards. Always remember, whenever you see something in somebody, first look within: the other may have functioned as a mirror. And try to change your inner being.

It has always happened that when you become silent the whole world becomes silent; when you become loving the whole world becomes loving. It reflects you, it echoes you; it is you, magnified a million-fold. But it is you: you are your world; there is no other world. This is the meaning of the Hindu concept, *maya*—illusion.

The whole world is illusory because it is just your projection. Once your projections disappear, then suddenly you become aware that that world has disappeared, and another world has arisen, the real. When you don't have anything to project then the real arises, that which is. Call it God, call it truth, or whatsoever you like; but the only way to know that truth, is to become aware of your projections. And in awareness they start dropping by and by.

The day is not far off when projections will disappear, if you can remain aware. Awareness is a tremendous fire: it burns all, root and all. It burns the very seeds. And only then, the truth is realized.

MATTHEW 22

35 Then one of them, which was a lawyer,
asked him a question,
tempting him, and saying,

36 Master,
which is the great commandment in the law?

37 Jesus said unto him,
Thou shalt love the Lord thy God
with all thy heart,
and with all thy soul,
and with all thy mind.

38 This is the first and great commandment.

39 And the second is like unto it,
Thou shalt love thy neighbour as thyself.

40 On these two commandments
hang all the law and the prophets.

7   The more you love, the more fear disappears. If you love totally, fear is absolutely absent.

*T*HESE TWO WORDS, law and love, are tremendously significant. They represent two types of mind: the polar opposites. The mind which is legal can never be loving, and the mind that loves can never be legal. The legal attitude is irreligious; it is political, social; and the attitude of love is non-political, non-social, individual, personal, religious. Moses, Manu, Marx, Mao, these are the legal minds: they have given the law to the world. Jesus, Krishna, Buddha, Lao Tzu, these are the people of love. They have not given a legal commandment to the world; they have given a totally different vision.

I have heard a story about Frederick the Great, the King of Prussia—he was a very legal mind. A woman came to him and complained about her husband. She said, "Your Majesty, my husband treats me very mean."

Frederick the Great said, "That is not my business."

But the woman persisted. She said, "Not only that, Your Majesty, he speaks ill of you also."

Frederick the Great said, "That is none of your business." This is the legal mind.

The legal mind is always thinking of law, never of love. The legal mind thinks of justice, but never of compassion; and a justice which is without compassion can never be just. A justice which has not compassion in it is bound to be unjust; and a compassion which may appear unjust cannot be unjust. The very nature of compassion is to be just. Justice follows compassion as a shadow. But compassion doesn't follow justice as a shadow, because compassion is the real thing, love is the real thing. Your shadow follows you; you don't follow your shadow. The shadow cannot be followed, the shadow has to follow. And this is one of the greatest controversies of human history: whether God is love, or law; whether he is just, or compassionate.

The legal mind says God is law. He is just. But the legal mind cannot know what God is, because God is another name for love. The legal mind cannot reach to that dimension. The legal mind always goes on throwing responsibility on somebody else: the society, the economic structure, the history. Always the other is responsible, for the legal mind. Love takes the responsibility on itself: it is always 'I' who is responsible, not you.

I have heard a Chinese parable. In Chuang Tzu's garden there was one rose-bush which used to flower much. Then suddenly it stopped flowering. Chuang Tzu became, of course, worried— he had always loved that rose-bush. He started showering his love on it, watching it more, taking more and more care. But nothing happened; the rose-bush remained barren, unblossomed. Weeks passed, and then months passed. Then one day Chuang Tzu thought that something had gone basically wrong. It seemed the rose-bush could not be helped, and he was just going to decide not to interfere, when the rose-bush spoke up. And the rose-bush said, "Sir, nothing is wrong with me—it is because of the wrong surroundings that I cannot produce flowers. Look at the soil; look at those rocks near me. They are destroying my roots. Look at the hot sun—it is so hot, burning hot. How can I flower? How can you expect me to? And, I am alone here; I need other rose-bushes as companions, as competitors. Only then can I flower."

Chuang Tzu put a shield on the rose-bush to protect it from the sun. The beautiful rocks that he had arranged at the side were removed; the soil was changed. But nothing happened. Weeks passed; then one day Chuang Tzu said, "Don't be hurt. Now let me tell you the truth. Nothing is wrong with the surroundings—something has gone wrong in your mind. You remind me of one of my disciples who is a lawyer, who always goes on throwing responsibility onto somebody else. And, because of that, he cannot change."

The rose-bush laughed, and said: "Sir, in fact that lawyer-disciple of yours—he has corrupted me also; I have been following him." And from the next day the rose-bush became different, became greener, and soon flowers were coming. The rocks were replaced, the shield was removed, and the surroundings were as of old. But bigger and bigger flowers were coming.

Once you understand that you are responsible, you start blossoming. Law is an excuse. It is cunningness, cunningness of the mind, so that you can always protect yourself, defend yourself. It is a defence. Love is vulnerable, law is a defence arrangement. When you love somebody, you don't talk law. When you love, law disappears, because love is the ultimate law; it needs no other law. It is enough unto itself; and when love protects you, you don't need any other protection. Don't be legal, otherwise you will miss all that is beautiful in life. Don't be a lawyer, be a lover; otherwise you will go on protecting yourself, and in the end you will find that there is nothing to protect—you have been protecting just an empty ego. And you can always find ways and means to protect the empty ego.

I have heard about one very famous artist, Oscar Wilde. His first play was dramatised. It failed completely; it was a flop. And when he came out of the theatre hall, friends asked, "How did it go?" He said, "It was a great success. The audience was a great failure."

This is the legal mind, always trying to protect one's ego, the empty ego—nothing but a soap bubble, hollow within, full of emptiness, and nothing in it. But the law goes on protecting. Remember, the moment you become legal, the moment you start looking at life through the law—maybe the law is that of the government, or the law is that of the churches, it makes no difference—the moment you start looking at life through the law, through the morality, the code, the scripture, the commandment, you start missing it. One needs to be vulnerable to know what life is; one needs to be totally open, insecure; one needs to be able to die in knowing it—only then one comes to know life. If you are afraid of death, you will never know life, because fear can never know. If you are unafraid of death, if you are ready to die to know, you will know life, eternal life, which never dies. Law is hidden fear, love is expressed fearlessness.

When you love, fear disappears—have you observed? When you love, there is no fear. If you love a person, fear disappears. The more you love, the more fear disappears. If you love totally, fear is absolutely absent: fear arises only when you don't love. When love does not exist, then the fear arises. Fear is absence of love; law is absence of love, because law is basically nothing but a defence of your inner trembling heart, of your inner trembling —you are afraid; you want to protect.

If the society is based on law, the society will remain continuously in fear. If the society is based on love, the fear disappears and the law is not needed—courts will not be needed; hell and heaven will not be needed. Hell is a legal attitude: all punishment is legal. The law says if you do wrong you will be punished; if you do right you will be rewarded. And then there are so-called religions—they say if you commit sin you will be thrown into hell. Just think about their hell. These people who have created the idea of hell must have been very deeply sadistic. The way they have arranged hell, they have made every arrangement possible to make you suffer.

I have heard about a priest who was teaching, and he came to talk about hell. He warmed up to the theme, and said, "There will be much fire, and you will be thrown into it. And there will be much trembling and gnashing of teeth." And an old woman stood up and she said, "Sir, I have lost my teeth." The priest said, "Don't be worried. False teeth will be provided."

They have made every arrangement to make you suffer—it comes out of a sadist's imagination. These people who have invented hell are dangerous. And they have invented heaven also: heaven for themselves and for those who follow them, hell for those who don't follow them and don't believe in them. But these are legal attitudes: the same attitude as punishment. And punishment has failed.

Crime cannot be stopped, it has not been stopped, by punishment. It goes on growing, because in fact the legal mind and the criminal mind are two aspects of the same coin; they are not different. All legal minds are basically criminal, and all criminal minds can become good legal minds—they have the potentiality. They are not two separate worlds; they are part of one world. Crime goes on increasing, and the law goes on becoming more and more complicated and complex.

By punishment man has not been changed; in fact, man has been more corrupted. Courts have not changed him; they have corrupted him more. And neither the concepts of reward, heaven, respectability, have been of any help, because hell depends on fear, and heaven depends on greed. Fear and greed, those are the problems. How can you change man through them? They are the diseases, and the legal mind goes on saying they are the medicines.

A totally different attitude is needed: the attitude of love.

Christ brings love to the world. He destroys law, the very basis
of it. That was his crime; that's why he was crucified—because
he was destroying the whole basis of this criminal society; he
was destroying the whole foundation rock of this criminal world,
the world of wars, and violence, and aggression. He gave a totally
new foundation stone. These few lines have to be understood as
deeply as possible.

> *Then one of them, which was a lawyer,*
> *asked him a question,*
> *tempting him, and saying . . .*

Tempting him . . . He wanted to pull him down into a legal
argument. There are many instances in Jesus' life where he had
been tempted to come down from the heights of love to the dark
valleys of law. And the people who tempted were very tricky.
Their questions were such that, if Jesus was not really a realized
one, he would have fallen a victim. They gave him what is called
in logic, dilemmas—whatsoever you answer, you will be caught.
If you say this, you will be caught; if you say the opposite, then
you will also be caught.

    You must have heard the famous story. He is sitting by the
side of the river; the crowd have come, and they have brought a
woman. And they say to him that this woman has committed
sin: "What do you say?" They tempted him; because it is said
in the old scripture that if a woman commits sin, she should be
stoned to death. Now they are giving two alternatives to Jesus.
If he says follow the scripture, then they will ask, "Where has
your concept of love, of compassion, gone? Can't you forgive
her? So that talk of love is just talk." Then he will be caught.
Or, if he says, "Forgive her," then they will say, "Then you are
against the scripture; and you have been saying to people, 'I
have come to fulfil the scripture, not to destroy it.'" This is
dilemma; now these are the only two alternatives.

    But the legal mind never knows that a man of love has also

a third alternative, which the legal mind cannot know about, because the legal mind can only think in opposites. Only two alternatives exist: yes or no. The legal mind does not know about the third alternative, which de Bono has called po—yes, no, and the third alternative is po: it is neither yes nor no; it is totally different.

Jesus is the first man in the world to say po. He didn't use the term; the term has been invented by de Bono. But he said po, he actually did it. He said to these people, to the crowd, that the scripture is right: one who has committed sin should be stoned to death. But... "Only those people amongst you who have never sinned, and never thought of committing sins, you should come forward. You should take stones in your hands and kill this woman." Now there was not a single one who had not committed sin, or who had not thought of committing it.

There may be people who have not committed sin, but they may be thinking continuously about it. In fact, they are bound to think about it. People who commit, think less about it: those who don't commit, continuously think and fantasise. And for the innermost core of your being, it makes no difference whether you think or you do.

By and by the crowd started disappearing. People who were standing in front disappeared to the back—the legal leaders of the society, the prominent citizens of the town, started disappearing. This man had used a third alternative. He didn't say yes, he didn't say no. He said, "Yes, kill the woman"—but only those who have never committed sin or thought about it, they should kill her. The crowd disappeared. Only Jesus was left with the woman. The woman fell at his feet and said, "I have really committed sin. I am a bad woman. You can punish me." Jesus said: "Who am I to judge? This is between you and your Lord God. This is something between you and God. Who am I to interfere? If you realize that you have done something wrong, don't do it again. God bless you."

Such situations were continuously repeated. The whole effort was to bring him into an argument where the legal mind can succeed. You cannot argue with the legal mind—if you argue you will be defeated because in argument the legal mind is very efficient. Whatsoever position you take up, it matters not; you will be defeated. Jesus could not be defeated because he never argued. This is one of the signs, one of the indications that he had attained to love. He remained on his peak; he never descended.

> *Then one of them, which was a lawyer,*
> *asked him a question,*
> *tempting him, and saying,*
> *Master,*
> *which is the great commandment in the law?*

That respect is false. He says, "Master," but that respect is not true. The legal respect is never true. Whenever you pay respect as an etiquette, as a social manner, if your respect is just because you have been taught to show respect—you respect your father because you have been told again and again, conditioned—then that respect is false. If you pay respect to your mother because you have been told that one should pay respect to the mother, then that respect is false. Unless it comes out of love, it is a false coin.

And love is an unconditioned feeling—you have never been taught anything about love. Love you have brought into the world with yourself; it has just come with you; it is your nature. Only when respect comes out of love is it true; otherwise it is a deception.

The lawyer said: *Master, which is the great commandment in the law?* Now, it is a very difficult question: which is the great commandment, which is the foremost commandment, which is the fundamental commandment in law? It is very difficult, because every law depends on other laws—they are interlinked. You cannot find the basic law, because no law is basic. They depend on each other; they are interdependent.

For example, if you ask somebody what is matter, he will say, "Not mind." Then ask him what is mind, and he will say, "Not matter." Both are undefined, both are indefinables, but you create a fallacy of definition. Asked what is matter, you say, "Not mind." The mind itself is undefined. You bring one indefinable to define something else—which is stupid, but on the surface looks very wise—it seems you have answered. Then you are asked what is mind, and you say, "Not matter." Neither mind is known, nor matter. Two unknowns are there, but you go on fooling yourself, and fooling others. The fundamental law is not known, cannot be known. It is not only unknown, it is unknowable; and all other laws are dependent on each other: for example, whether truth is the fundamental law, or non-violence.

In India it has been one of the controversies: which is basic—non-violence or truth? If you are in a situation where you have to choose between truth or non-violence—if you say the truth, then there will be violence; if you don't say the truth, the violence can be avoided. What will you do? Will you say the truth, and help the violence to be committed?

For example, you are standing at a crossroad, and a group of policemen come. And they ask you, "Have you seen a man pass along this road? He has to be caught and killed. He has escaped from prison. He is sentenced to death." You have seen the man. You can say, "Yes," and be true; but then you will be responsible for the death of that man. You can say you have not seen him, or you can even give a wrong direction; then that man is saved. You remained non-violent, but you became untrue. What will you do? It seems impossible to choose, almost impossible. Which law is the most fundamental?

> *Jesus said unto him,*
> *Thou shalt love the Lord thy God*
> *with all thy heart,*
> *and with all thy soul,*
> *and with all thy mind.*

This is po: he is not answering the question at all; he is answering something else. He is not getting down to the legal world; he remains perched on his peak of love. He says,

> *This is the first and great commandment.*

Love thy God with all thy heart, all thy mind, and all thy soul. The question was about law, and the answer is about love. In fact, he has not answered the question; or, you can say he has answered the question because this is the only answer, there can be no other answer.

This has to be understood. Only from a higher plane can the question of a lower plane be answered; remaining on the same plane, the answer is impossible. For example, from where you are the question arises, many questions arise. If you ask a person who remains on the same plane as you, he cannot answer you. His answers may look relevant, but cannot be relevant, because he is also in the same situation as you.

It is like a madman helping another madman, the blind leading the blind, a confused man helping another confused man to attain to clarity. More muddledness, more confusion will happen out of it. That's what has happened in the world—everybody is advising everybody else. Nothing is cheaper than advice; in fact, it costs nothing—just for the asking, and everybody is ready to give you advice. Neither you think about it, nor those who are giving you advice, that they exist on the same plane, that their advice is simply useless; or, it can be even harmful. Only somebody who is on a higher plane than you can be of any help; one who has a clearer perception, a deeper clarity, a more crystallised being—only he can answer your questions.

have heard—it happened once: In a certain city in Tibet, wisdom was sold. A man who wanted to become wise went to the marketplace. There were many shops, and in every shop wisdom was sold. And it was plentiful; in fact so much so that it was very cheap. So he purchased thousands of wisdom bits. He came home loaded with many bullock carts. He became wise. Then he used to visit his friends to show the wisdom, because when you have it, you have to show it; otherwise what is its use? A wisdom that is borrowed or purchased can have only one function—that of exhibition. It cannot be of any use to you; you can just use it as a decoration. But those friends had also purchased from the same market, and everybody was wise. In that town it was difficult to find a foolish man, because all fools had purchased. They discussed, they argued; every day they would meet and hurt each other by their arguments, and everybody would try to prove that 'my' view was right. And nobody was ready to listen to anybody. They created much confusion, much anger, much hostility. And they enjoyed it—that fiery exchange of hostility—they became addicted to it.

But this man, by and by, became fed up with the whole nonsense. He started thinking, "I was better before I purchased these wisdom bits. My mind is more burdened; I am more tense; I cannot sleep, with continuous arguments and discussions leading nowhere, moving in vicious circles." So he went to a wise man and asked what he should do. The wise man said, "It is natural. When people exist on the same plane, they cannot help each other. They can only fight, and they can only try to help each other; but they will basically cause harm. You throw away all this nonsense that you call wisdom. Wisdom cannot be purchased; one has to grow into it." And he said one very profound thing: he said, "If you purchase wisdom, if you learn from somebody else, if you borrow it, if it is not your own, then you will always be in trouble; because everything that you can borrow has its opposite. But if you grow in it, then it has no opposite to it."

Let me explain it to you. Every law has its opposite, because law is borrowed wisdom. Love has not its opposite—if it has, then it is not love at all. Every law has its opposite; every law can be argued against, every proof can be disproved, and there is no argument which is absolute or final.

I used to know a very great lawyer. He founded a university in India—he was one of the topmost men in his profession. Once it happened: he was a little absent-minded, and he was fighting a case in the Privy Council. Two Indian States were fighting. He forgot—he had drunk too much the night before and he had a hangover. And when he went to the Privy Council, he forgot for whom he was fighting. So he started arguing for the opposite party; and he was a great lawyer, so he argued well. His assistant became very much worried—what should he do? He pulled his coat many times, but he wouldn't listen; he was so much in the debate. When there was a break for tea, the assistant said, "You have destroyed the whole thing. You are arguing against yourself." But the lawyer didn't say anything. When the court started again, he said, "Up to now, I was giving you the arguments for the opposite party. Now I will give the arguments for my party." And he won the case.

Every law has its opposite; every argument has its opposite. Every proof, if it is only logical, has its opposite. Only love has no opposite to it. The lawyer asked Jesus something; Jesus answered something else. As if the lawyer was only asking for stones, and Jesus gave him diamonds. In a way, it is irrelevant. In another way, in a deeper way, this is the only way it should be. Diamonds were not asked for—the lawyer had no idea about those diamonds; he was only asking about some coloured stones, at the most, semi-precious. Jesus gave him diamonds—tremendously valuable; he was asking about law, and Jesus talked about love.

Always remember it: whenever you come to an enlightened man, whatsoever you say is not the point. He talks out of his heart. In fact, he does not answer your questions; he answers you, your deepest need, about which you yourself are not aware.

It happens so many times when I am answering your questions. Many times you feel as if your question has not been answered. I know it; I am aware of it. It need not be answered. But through your question I can feel a deep urge, a deep enquiry, about which you yourself are not aware. You cannot be aware in the state you are in—in your unconsciousness you can ask only wrong questions. In my awareness I can answer only right answers. I will repeat: in your sleep you can ask only wrong questions; in my awareness I can answer only right answers. On the surface it will look absurd.

There are three possibilities of dialogue: one, two ignorant persons talking. Much talking goes on, but nothing happens out of it; it is just bogus. They talk, but they don't mean what they are saying, they are not even aware of what they are saying—it is just an occupation; it feels good to be occupied. They are talking like mechanical things, two computers talking. Then there is the possibility of two enlightened persons talking. They don't talk; there is no need to talk. The communion is silent; they understand each other without the words. Two ignorant persons talking—too many words, and no understanding. Two enlightened persons meeting—no words, only understanding.

The first situation happens every day, millions of times all over the earth; the second situation happens rarely after thousands and thousands of years—rarely does it happen that two enlightened persons meet.

There is a third possibility—one enlightened person talking to an unenlightened person. Then there are two planes: one is on the earth, the other is in the sky; one is moving in a bullock cart, the other is flying in an aeroplane. The person on the earth asks one thing and the person in the sky answers something

else. But this is the only way, this is the only way the person on
the earth can be helped. The lawyer had asked about the law.
He had asked,

> *Master,*
> *which is the great commandment in the law?*

He is not asking about love; Jesus is trying to seduce him
towards love—he has changed the whole pattern. Once it is in
Jesus' hands, then he will take you into a dimension you know
not, into the unknown, into the unknowable.

> *Jesus said unto him,*
> *Thou shalt love the Lord thy God*
> *with all thy heart,*
> *and with all thy soul,*
> *and with all thy mind.*

With all thy heart means with all thy feelings. That is what
prayer is. When all your feelings are together, integrated into
one unity, it is prayer. Prayer is your total heart, throbbing with
the desire of the unknown, throbbing with a deep urge, a deep
enquiry for the unknown, each beat of your heart devoted.

With all thy mind: that is the meaning of meditation, when
all your thoughts have become one. When all your thoughts
become one, thinking disappears; when all your feelings become
one, feeling disappears. When your feelings are many, you are
sentimental; when your feelings are one, all sentimentality disappears—you are full of heart, but without any sentimentality.
Prayer is not sentimentalism. Prayer is such a harmony of feelings, such a total unity of feelings that the quality of the feelings
immediately changes. Just as you put water on to heat, it goes
on becoming warmer, warmer, hot, more hot—up to 99° it is
still water. Then the 100° comes, and suddenly there is a transformation. The water is no more water, it starts evaporating;
and the quality immediately changes. The water has a quality to

flow downwards: when it evaporates, the vapour has a quality to float upwards. The dimension has changed.

When you live in feelings, so many feelings, you are just a confusion, a madhouse. When all the feelings are integrated, there comes a moment of transformation. When they all become one, you are at the 100° point, the evaporating point. Immediately the nature of the feelings disappears. The old down-flowing is no more there; you start evaporating like vapour towards the sky. That is what prayer is.

And the same thing happens when all your thoughts are one —thinking stops. When thoughts are many, thinking is possible; when thoughts are one, then there comes a moment that this one-ness of thought becomes almost synonymous with no-thought. To have one thought is to have no thought, because the one cannot exist alone. The one can exist only with the many, the one can exist only in a crowd. When the crowd has disappeared, the one also disappears, and there comes a state of no-thought.

So Jesus, in his small sentence, has condensed the whole of religion.

Thou shalt love the Lord thy God with all thy heart: this is what prayer is all about.

With all thy mind: that is what meditation is all about.

And with all thy soul: the soul is the transcendence of thinking and feeling. The soul is beyond prayer and beyond meditation. The soul is your nature—it is the transcendental consciousness in you. Look at yourself as a triangle—on the lower base, feeling, thinking. But feeling and thinking are the only two that you have been feeling up to now; you don't know the third. The third can be known only when the feeling becomes prayer, and starts moving upwards, and thinking becomes meditation, and starts moving upwards. Then prayer and meditation meet at a point—that point is soul. Somewhere your heart and your mind meet: that is you, that is a beyondness. That's what Jesus calls the soul.

This is the first and great commandment.

Now he is using the language of the lawyer. He has said whatsoever he wanted to say; now he comes to the language of the lawyer. The first sentence belongs to Jesus' plane; the second sentence belongs to the lawyer's plane. And he has tried to create a bridge between the two.

This is the first and the great commandment: love is the first and the great commandment. In fact, love is not a commandment at all, because you cannot be commanded to love; you cannot be ordered to love, you cannot be forced to love, you cannot manage and control love. Love is bigger than you, higher than you—how can you control it? And if you are commanded to love, if somebody comes just as they do in the army: "Right turn! Left turn!"—and somebody comes and says, "Love!" what can you do? 'Right turn' is okay. 'Left turn' is okay. But 'Love turn'?—you don't know where to turn, where to go; you don't know that way—it cannot be commanded.

Yes, you can pretend; you can act. That's what has happened on this earth. The greatest curse that has happened on this earth is that love has been forced. From the very childhood everybody is taught to love, as if love can be taught. 'Love your mother', 'Love your father', 'Love your brothers', 'Love your sisters', love this, love that: and the child starts trying—because how can the child know that love cannot be an act? It is a happening.

*J*ust the other night I was saying . . . once it happened: A musician was playing on his organ—just sitting idle, with nothing to do; in a playful mood, not serious at all—in fun. Suddenly something happened for which he had been waiting his whole life. He struck a chord. For that chord he had been waiting, and waiting, and waiting. He had tried his utmost and he had never been able to manage it; and suddenly it was there . . . and he had just been fingering the keys. He was thrilled, ecstatic. He danced. And then he tried again. But he could not get it again. He tried hard—the harder he tried, the more frustrated he was. For months he became almost mad. He tried and tried, day and night; and the more he tried, the further away it looked. In fact, after a few weeks he started to wonder if it had ever happened, or if he had imagined it. The memory of it had also gone so far away that he started thinking, "Maybe I simply dreamt about it, and it has not happened." Then he dropped the whole subject. Then he forgot about it.

Again one day after a few months, he was just sitting at the organ, fingering the keys. Again it was there; again it happened. He was thrilled; he was ecstatic. But now he understood—it happened only when he was not there. Then he never tried; then he never tried to bring it back. It started to happen almost every day. It started to happen, by and by, whenever he touched the keys. It became a natural flow.

Love is just like that. You cannot force it. You have been missing because you have been trying too hard. The more I look and observe you, the more I feel your desert-like state. Everybody is in search of love. You may call it God, you may call it something else; but deep down I know you are in search of love. But you have become incapable, not because you have not tried, but because you have tried too hard.

Love is a happening; it cannot be commanded. Because you have been commanded to love, your love has been falsified from the very beginning, poisoned from the very source. Never say to a child—never commit this sin—never say to a child, "Love your mother." Love the child, and let love happen. Don't say, "Love. Love me, because I am your mother, or I am your father. Love me." Don't make it a commandment; otherwise your child will miss for ever and ever. Just love him. In a loving milieu, one day suddenly the chord just happens, the harmony is found in the innermost organ of your being. Something starts; some melody, some harmony arises, and then you know that it is your nature. But then you never try to do it; then you simply relax and allow it to be.

This is the first and great commandment. Jesus is using the language of the lawyer, because he is answering him; otherwise love is not a commandment, and cannot be a commandment.

And the second is like unto it,
Thou shalt love thy neighbour as thyself.

The first is, love thy God. God means the total, the tao, the brahma. God is not a very good word; tao is far better—the total, the whole, the existence—love existence. That is the first, the most fundamental.

And the second is like unto it,
Thou shalt love thy neighbour as thyself.

... because it is difficult to find God, and it is difficult to love God, if you have not found him already. How can you love God, who is unknown? How can you love the unknown? You need some bridge, you need some familiarity. How can you love God? It looks absurd; it is absurd. Hence the second commandment.

And the second is like unto it,
Thou shalt love thy neighbour as thyself.

I was reading a story—I liked it. A learned man asked Rabbi Abraham, "They say that you give people mysterious drugs, and that your drugs are effective. Give me one, that I may attain to the fear of God."

"I don't know any drug for the fear of God," said the Rabbi. "But, if you like, I can give you one for the love of God."

"That is even better!" cried the scholar. "Just you give it to me."

"It is the love of one's fellow men," answered the Rabbi.

If you really want to love God, you have to start by loving

your fellow men, because that is the nearest God is to you. And by and by, ripples of your love can go on expanding. Love is like a pebble thrown into a silent lake: ripples arise, and then they start spreading to the faraway shores. But—first the touch of the pebble on the lake; close to the pebble they arise, and then far and far away they spread.

First, you will have to love those who are like you—because you know them, because at least you can feel a certain familiarity, a certain at-homeness with them. Then the love can go on expanding. Then you can love animals, then you can love trees, then you can love rocks. And then only can you love existence as such, not before then.

So, if you can love human beings, you have taken the first step. But just the opposite has been happening on this unfortunate earth—people love God, and kill human beings. In fact, they say because they love God so much, they have to kill. Christians kill Mohammedans, Mohammedans kill Christians, Hindus kill Mohammedans, Mohammedans kill Hindus, because they all love God—in the name of God, they kill human beings.

Their gods are false. Because if your God is true, if you have really known what God means, if you have realised even a bit, if you have even attained to just a glimpse of what God is, you will love human beings; you will love animals, you will love trees, you will love rocks—you will Love. Love will become your natural state of being. And if you cannot love human beings, don't be deceived—then no temple is going to help you.

Just two or three days before, one beautiful woman, a rare person, came to see me. Her whole life she has been a humanist, not believing in God, a no-sayer. She told me, "I am surprised that I am here." Her surprise is natural. She had never been to any temple, to any church, to the so-called religious people; and then she has come here. And not only that—she wanted to be initiated into sannyas. She could not believe herself—what was happening. But I could look into her. She has been able to come to me because she has loved human beings. She has taken the first step towards the temple. She may not have gone to any temple—that is not needed. She may not have ever thought about God—that is not needed. But she has taken an authentic step; she has loved human beings. She has been a no-sayer, but that is the basis for saying yes. She has earned her sannyas.

There are two types of people who come to me and want to be initiated: a few who have not earned it—she has earned it. Some will start earning it only after they have taken sannyas—for them it is a beginning. But for that old woman it is not a beginning, it is a culmination. She has arrived. Her whole life has been a preparation for it. She said no. To say yes to human beings she denied God: perfectly good—as it should be. Say no to God, but never say no to human beings, because if you say no to human beings, the path is cut; then you will never be able to reach God. Say no to the church, to the temple; there is no problem about it. But never say no to love, because that is the real temple. All other temples are just false coins, pseudo-images, not authentic. There is only one authentic temple, and that temple is love. Never say no to love—you will find God; God cannot hide for long.

The second commandment, Jesus says,

Thou shalt love thy neighbour as thyself.

. . . because, in fact, all humanity is you, in many faces and in many forms. Can't you see it—that your neighbour is nobody else than you, your own being in a different shape and form?

Many rivers in the world are named after colours. In China we have the Yellow River; somewhere in South Africa they have the Red River; in the U.S., I have heard, they have the White River, the Green River, the Purple River. In Spain they have a river, the Rio Tinto—it has three names. Somewhere it is known as the Green River, somewhere as the Red River, somewhere as the White River. The river itself has no colour; water is colourless, but the river takes the colour of the terrain it passes through, the colour of the shrubbery on the banks. If it passes a desert, of course it has a different colour; if it passes through a forest, the forest is reflected—the shrubbery, the greenery—it has a different colour. If it passes through a terrain where the mud is yellow, it becomes yellow. But no river has any colour. And every river, whether it is called white, or green, or yellow, reaches naturally to its end, to its destiny, falls into the ocean, and becomes oceanic.

Your differences are because of your terrain. Your colours are different because of your terrain. But your innermost quality of being is colourless; it is the same. Somebody is black, a negro; somebody is white, an Englishman; somebody is just in the middle, an Indian; somebody is yellow, a Chinese—so many colours. But remember, these are the colours of the terrain of the body you pass through. They are not your colours; you are colourless.

In India, we have a name for the sannyasin—we call him *viragi*. That means colourless. *Rag* means colour; *virag* means colourlessness; and *viragi* is one who has come to know his colourless being.

You are not the body; neither are you the mind, nor are you the heart. Your mind differs, because it has been conditioned differently; your body is different, because it has come through a different terrain, through a different heredity; but you are not different.

Jesus says: *Thou shalt love thy neighbour as thyself.* As you love yourself, love your neighbour. And one thing very basic, which Christians have completely forgotten—Jesus says, "Love thyself," and, "Love thy neighbour as thyself."

Unless you love yourself, you cannot love your neighbour.

And the so-called Christianity has been teaching you hatred towards yourself, condemnation towards yourself. Love yourself, because you are the nearest to God. It is there that the first ripple has to arise. Love yourself. Self-love is the most fundamental thing—if you ever want to be religious, self-love is the basis. And all so-called religions go on teaching you self-hatred: "Condemn yourself, you are a sinner, guilty—this and that— you are worthless."

You are not a sinner. They have made you so. You are not guilty. They have given you wrong interpretations of life. Accept yourself, and love yourself. Only then can you love your neighbour, otherwise there is no possibility. If you don't love yourself, how can you love another being? I teach you self-love. At least do that; if you cannot do anything else—love yourself. And out of your self-love, by and by you will see love is starting to flow; it is expanding; it is reaching to the neighbours.

The whole problem today is that you hate yourself and you want to love somebody else, which is impossible. And the other also hates himself, and he wants to love you. That lesson has to be learned first within yourself.

If you ask Freud and the psychoanalysts, they have come to discover a very basic thing. They say—first, the child is auto-erotic, masturbatory; the child loves himself. Then the child becomes homosexual—the boys love boys and want to play with boys; girls want to play with girls, and they don't want to mix with each other. And then arises heterosexuality—the boy wants to mix, and love a girl; a girl wants to meet a boy and love. First, auto-erotic, then homo-erotic, then hetero-erotic—this is about sex. The same is true about love.

First, you love yourself. Then you love your neighbour, other human beings. And then you move beyond: you love existence. But the basis is you. So don't condemn yourself; don't reject yourself. Accept. God has taken abode in you. He has loved you so much, that's why he has taken abode in you. He has made a temple of you; he lives in you. If you reject yourself, you reject the nearest to God that you can find. If you reject the nearest, it is impossible that you will love the faraway.

When Jesus says: *Thou shalt love thy neighbour as thyself*, he is saying two things: first, love thyself, so that you can be capable of loving thy neighbour.

> *On these two commandments*
> *hang all the law and the prophets.*

In fact it is one commandment, Love. Love is the one and only order of things. If you have understood love, you have understood all. If you have not understood love, you may know many things, but all that knowledge is simply rot. Throw it on a rubbish heap and forget all about it. Start from the very beginning. Be a child again, and start loving yourself again.

Your lake, as I see it, has no ripples. The first pebble of love has not fallen in it.

I have heard a Danish story. Remember it—let it become part of your mindfulness. The story tells about a spider who lived high up in the rafters of an old barn. One day he let himself down by a long thread to a lower beam, where he found the flies were more plentiful and more easily caught. He therefore decided to live permanently at this lower level, and spun himself a comfortable web there. But one day he happened to notice the line down which he had come, stretching away into the darkness above. "I don't need this any more," he said. "It only gets in the way." He snapped it, and with it destroyed his whole web, which needed it for support.

This is the story of man also. A thread joins you with the ultimate, the highest; call it God. You may have completely forgotten that you have descended from there. You come from God, and you have to go back to him. Everything goes

back to the original source; it has to be so. Then the circle
is complete, and one is fulfilled. And you may even feel like
this spider, that the thread that joins you to the highest comes
in the way. Many times because of it you cannot do many
things: again and again it comes in the way. You cannot be
violent as you would like to be; you cannot be aggressive as you
would like to be; you cannot hate as much as you would like
to hate—the line comes again and again in the way. And sometimes you may feel like this spider: to cut it, to snap at it, so that
your path is clear.

That's what Nietzsche says: "God is dead." He snapped at
it. But immediately Nietzsche became mad. The moment he
said, "God is dead," he became mad, because then you are cut
away from the original source of all life. Then you are starved
of something very vital, essential. Then you miss something,
for you had become completely oblivious that it was the very
base. The spider snapped at the thread, and with it destroyed his
whole web, which needed it for support.

Wherever you are, in your darkest night, a ray of light is
still joined with you from God, from existence. That is your
life; that's how you are alive. Find out that thread, because that
is going to be the way back home.

On 5th June, 1910, O'Henry was dying. It was getting dark.
Friends were surrounding him. Suddenly he opened his eyes
and said, "Put the light up. I don't want to go home in darkness." The light was put up; he closed his eyes, smiled, and
disappeared.

The thread that is joining you, the single ray of life that is
making you alive, is the way back home. Howsoever far you have
gone, you are still joined with God—otherwise it would not be
possible. You may have forgotten him, but he has not forgotten
you; and that is the real thing that matters.

Try to find out something in you which joins you to existence.

Search for it, and you will come to the commandment Jesus is talking about. If you search, you will come to know it is love, not knowledge, that joins you to existence; not riches, not power, not fame—it is love that joins you to existence. And whenever you feel love, you are tremendously happy, because more and more life becomes available to you.

Jesus, or a Buddha, both are like a honey-bee. The honey-bee goes and finds beautiful flowers in a valley. She comes back, she dances a dance of ecstasy near her friends to tell them that she has found a beautiful valley full of flowers. Come, follow me. A Jesus is just a honey-bee who has found the original source of life: a valley of beautiful flowers, flowers of eternity. He comes and dances near you to give you the message: Come, follow me.

If you try to understand and seek within you, you will find it is love that is the most significant, most essential thing in your being. Don't starve it. Help it to grow, so that it can become a big tree; so that birds of heaven can take shelter in you; so that in your love, tired travellers on the path can rest; so that you can share your love; so that you can also become a honey-bee. In your esctasy, you can also tell people to come and follow you. Each and everyone has to become a Jesus one day, and don't be contented for less. Unless you become a Jesus, you cannot be a Christian. If you are satisfied by being a Christian, you are fooling yourself. Be a Jesus—less than that is not worthwhile. And you can be, because in fact you are. Only a recognition . . . just a recognition.

8 *I bring the greatest synthesis that is possible in the world to you, the synthesis of love and meditation.*

I often desire to have an isolated, secure place to allow surrender. Meditations several hours a day, going deeper and deeper without distraction. As I understand, most yoga masters teach that withdrawal from the world is necessary for a period of time, once kundalini starts rising, until one is finally established in samadhi; at which time one can really be in the world, but not of it. Your teaching seems to be different: to engage in the world while the transformation is occurring. If this is so, how do I avoid the distraction of maya before I clearly see the reality?

THE FIRST THING: the ego always seeks isolation, in a thousand and one ways. When you become very rich, you become isolated. When you become politically very powerful, you become isolated. An Adolf Hitler is alone, more alone than a yogi in the Himalayas. He has no friends, nobody equal to him; he has no relationships. A very rich man reaches to a

Himalayan peak, where he is alone. Hence one seeks riches, hence one seeks political power.

The ego is always in search of isolation, because when you are alone, only the ego remains; the ego becomes the whole world. Then there is nobody to fight with your ego; there is nobody to humiliate you; there is nobody with whom you can compare yourself. You become supreme in your own eyes. You can believe in your ego absolutely; there will be no distraction.

I am against isolation. In fact you have to dissolve the ego, not to isolate it. You are not to become an island, independent, separate from the whole: you have to become a part of the continent, one with it. How can you be one with reality in isolation? The reality needs participation, not isolation. That's why the greatest *samadhi* occurs in love, not in isolation. And the greatest of yoga is love, because in love you have to dissolve yourself, in love you have to die, in love you have to melt, merge.

I teach love, not isolation. Isolation is the way of the world, not the way of religion. But it happens: you have been seeking riches, political power, possessions; then you become frustrated; then you turn to the Himalayas—you renounce the world. You don't renounce the ego, you renounce the world. I teach you: renounce the ego, don't renounce the world.

The ego is very subtle. You could not attain to political power, then you try to attain to religious power. You call it *kundalini*, but still it is power, still it is something that will make you separate, unique, independent, an island. If your religion is also a search for power, then isolation is needed.

But religion is not a search for power; it is a search for silence. It is a search for peace; it is a search for inner poverty—what Jesus calls 'poor in spirit'. It is a search to be, in such a way that there is no difference between to be and not to be. Non-being becomes your only being.

This is possible not through independence, this is possible only if you realize interdependence. These three words have to be remembered: dependence, independence, and interdependence. Dependent you are; independence you seek; interdependence I teach. Dependent you are, because everywhere you will feel you are dependent, everywhere a limitation comes in. If you love somebody you become dependent on him or on her. Everywhere life brings dependence. Then the idea arises that in the world you can never be independent. Escape from the world. You can escape, but independent you can never be: you can only be deceived. Even in the Himalayas you are not independent; you are still dependent on the sun. If the sun does not rise, you will be dead immediately. You will be dependent on the oxygen and air: if the oxygen disappears, you will be dead. You will be dependent on water; you will be dependent on a thousand and one things.

Dependence has to be understood, not to be avoided. If you understand dependence, you will understand immediately that hidden behind it is interdependence. Dependence is just a misinterpretation. Those who have known have also known that you are not dependent on the sun; the sun is also dependent on you. Without you the sun cannot be, as you cannot be without the sun. Even a small blade of grass will be missed from existence; the existence will never be complete without it. A gap, something missing, will be there.

So don't think that the stars are great, and a blade of grass is very small and tiny. In existence, nothing is great and nothing is small, because existence is one.

This is what is meant by ecology: interdependence. And ecology is not only of this earth, it is of the totality. Ecology is a spiritual phenomenon.

You are misinterpreting. You are interpreting interdependence as dependence. That is a wrong notion, and because of that wrong notion, a wrong desire arises: how to be independent. Out of one error another error arises. You cannot be; and if somebody teaches you independence—there are people who

teach this—they are teaching sheer stupidity. You are part, you
are one with the whole, you are a wave in the ocean. The wave
cannot be independent. How can you take the wave apart
from the ocean? And I tell you, the ocean also cannot be separate
from the wave. Without waves the ocean will also disappear.
The waves cannot be without the ocean; the ocean cannot be
without the waves, because waves are nothing but the ocean
waving. Because of language the separation arises. You say the
waves and the ocean; in fact, there are not the waves and the
ocean, it is all one—the ocean waving. Waves are not things . . .
a process, a movement, a breathing of the ocean. You and your
breathing are not two things: you are the breathing, the breathing is you. You breathe, and the breathing breathes you—they
are inseparable.

*L*ife is one. For this oneness, interdependence, God is
another name. Love is still another name, and even better
than God, because God has been destroyed by the theologians.
Love is still pure and virgin.

So the first thing to be understood: I don't teach isolation,
because I don't teach the ego. Your so-called yoga masters are
all more or less egoists. Once a man came to me, and he thought
he was a great seeker. The ego finds new ways to be fulfilled.
He was a great seeker, and he was very old. He told me that
throughout his whole life he had been seeking a perfect master,
the greatest in the world, because he could not be satisfied with
anything less than that. I asked him, "Could you find him?"
He said, "Yes, I met many, but I had to leave them. A few were
self-deceived; a few were deceiving others; a few were mad;
a few were simply idiots; a few were greedy, exploiters; a few
were just parrots, repeating the Vedas and the Upanishads. And
many other wrong sorts of guides I met. But then," his eyes
sparkled, and he said, "I came across a man who was a perfect

master, and I immediately spoke up and told him, 'You are the
greatest master in the world.'" I asked this seeker, "When did
you say this to him?" He said, "When he told me that I was the
most perfect disciple in the world . . . immediately."

The ego goes on seeking different ways to be enhanced. In
the name of yoga many ego-trips go on. Don't become a part
of it. I don't teach isolation, because I want you to leave the ego,
and not the world. The world is not the problem. The world is
tremendously beautiful; it is pure joy; nothing is wrong in it.
Something is wrong in you, not in the world. Drop that wrong-
ness in you; don't renounce the world. I teach you to celebrate
the world, not to renounce it. I affirm life, and affirm it unconditionally; and I say to you that those who tell you to renounce
it are the poisoners, and that from the very beginning they are
teaching you something absolutely wrong. They are saying
something is wrong in the world: they call it *maya*. I call you
maya—not the world. The ego is the only *maya*, the only
illusion—not these trees, they are simply beautiful; not these
flowers, not these birds, not this sky, not this sun, these stars—
no, they are simply beautiful; they are divine and holy.

You are the *maya*. So, if you want to leave anything, leave
yourself. If you want to renounce anything, renounce yourself.
And the only way, the only way to renounce oneself is to celebrate. Because whenever you are happy, you are not; whenever
you are sad, you are; whenever you are depressed, you are;
whenever you are delighting, you are not. In bliss, in ecstasy,
you disappear. In sadness and sorrow, you again appear. Watch.
When you laugh, you are not. In real laughter, you simply are
not. It comes out from somewhere you know not of. It comes
from beyond you. You don't laugh: when laughter is there,
you are not.

Dance. When the dance really possesses you, when there
really is a dance, the dancer is no more, the dancer has disappeared; he doesn't exist. The dance is so tremendously real

that the unreal has to disappear before it. The unreal cannot face
the real; the false cannot confront the real; the lie cannot face
the truth; the darkness cannot encounter light. When the real
arises—and the real is when you are part of the whole, whether
in laughter, in dancing, in love—whenever you are part of the
whole, the real is. Separate, you are *maya*. One with the whole,
you are God.

   I often desire to have an isolated, secure place to allow surrender.
When you are alone, a false type of 'religiosity' arises. Because
whenever you are alone, there is nobody to provoke your anger,
nobody to create an opportunity where you can become sad,
nobody to bring your own false faces before you. You are alone:
anger does not arise. Not that anger has disappeared—simply the
situation for anger is not there. You are full of anger, but nobody
is there to insult you, to hurt you. Only the opportunity is
missing. Come back to the world: live fifty years in the Himalayas
—when you come back to the world, immediately you will
find anger is there, as fresh as ever; even maybe more powerful
now, because of fifty years accumulated anger, accumulated
poison. Then one becomes afraid to come back to the world.

   Go to the Himalayas: you will see many people hanging
around there. Cowards, they cannot come back to the world.
What sort of purity is this, which is afraid? What sort of celibacy
is this, which is afraid? What sort of reality is this, which is
afraid of *maya*, of illusion? What sort of light is this, which is
afraid of darkness: that if it comes to the dark, the darkness will
be powerful and may destroy it? Has darkness ever destroyed
any light? But they go on hanging around. The more they hang
around there, the more they become incapable of coming back
to the world—because there in the Himalayas they can have
their beautiful image: nobody else to destroy it. In the world
it is difficult. Somebody, from somewhere, treads on your toe;
somebody, from somewhere, hurts you. You have to drop anger.
My whole effort is so that you change. Don't try to change the

scene, please change yourself. The change of the scene is not going to help anybody; it has never helped anybody.

And you think . . . *meditation several hours a day*. Even if you meditate twenty-four hours a day it is not going to help unless meditation becomes a way of life—not that you meditate. Whether you meditate one hour, or two hours, or three hours, or six hours, or many hours—you may meditate twenty-four hours: you will go mad, but you will not attain to *samadhi*.

Samadhi is when you completely forget what meditation is. You don't meditate; just the way you live is meditative. The way you move, the way you walk, the way you eat: that becomes meditative. Meditation becomes a quality of your life; it is not a question of quantity. Don't be quantitative. Don't think that if you meditate more, then more meditation will happen to you . . . foolish. The more is not the question—quality, not quantity.

Meditation is not money that you can go on gathering and piling up. Meditation is a way of being: you don't pile it up, you cannot accumulate it, it is not a wealth. It is the way you are.

So whatsoever you are doing here are really not meditations. They are just situations through which I would like you to see; they are just preparations for the meditation. We call them meditations, because they prepare you for the right meditation. That is just clearing the ground, just cleansing the ground: they are not real meditations, because real meditations cannot be done, as real love cannot be done. It happens. You are simply cleaning your mindbody; you are purifying yourself so that you can become a vehicle, so that you can be possessed. Then whatsoever you do, you do meditatively.

There have been stories of people who were robbers, or butchers, who have attained to enlightenment. But they attained, because whatsoever they did was meditative. I have heard one taoist story: One Emperor of China had a butcher; and he always loved to see him whenever he came to kill the animals for his kitchen. The Emperor would come and see and watch, because the whole thing was so beautiful—such an ugly thing, but the butcher was so beautiful. He did it as if he was doing a prayer; he did it as if he was in deep ecstasy. And for thirty years the Emperor watched and watched, and he was never fed up. Every day he waited with great excitement: the butcher would be coming. The butcher carried a certain climate around him, as if he was going to the temple to pray to God— and he was just going to kill animals. First he would pray; then he would talk to the animal; then he would thank the animal. And when he killed the animal, each of his gestures had a tre- mendous beauty of its own. The Emperor used to watch.

One day he asked, "I have been watching you for twenty years. I am never fed up; every day I wait excitedly—I don't wait so excitedly for anything else in the twenty-four hours. What is the secret of it?" The butcher said, "Because it is medita- tion for me. I am a butcher: that is the way God has willed me to be. I was born the son of a butcher: that's how God has willed me to be. This is my life, and I have made it a meditation. If God wants me to be a butcher, let it be so. But I should be medi- tative; so this is my meditation. I go into deep ecstasy; it is not just an activity: it is an act of love. God is there in the animal, God is in me; and God wants to kill God himself. Perfectly okay. Who am I to interfere? I simply become a vehicle; I am simply possessed."

There are stories of people who were robbers and thieves, who have also attained. What was their secret? Just the same. And I know people who have lived in a Himalayan retreat for their whole life, and have not attained to anything. It is not a question of quantity—how much you do. The question is how you do it—not how much: what quality you bring to it. You can just walk and it can be meditative; you can just sit and it can be meditative; you can eat and it can be meditative; and you can just take a shower and it can be meditative. Try to understand this.

Meditation should become a climate around you, a milieu in which you live. And wherever you go, you carry your climate. This is my whole effort: that's why I don't send you to isolation, I don't send you to some mountains so that you can meditate the whole day; because that would give you a wrong notion about it, the notion of quantity.

Going deeper and deeper without distraction: you can never go deeper and deeper if you don't understand what distraction is. If you are trying to avoid distraction, you can never go deeper; because wherever you are, the distraction will follow you— because it is in you.

I will tell you one story: One man was very much distracted by his wife, because whenever he meditated the wife would talk loudly, or walk and close doors so loudly that plates would start falling; and he was very much distracted. So he left the house. He went into a forest. But then animals and crows started distracting him. Sometimes it was also happening that there was no distraction—then this would become the distraction. What is the matter?—there is no distraction. Absolute silence, and he would be distracted: what is happening? Have all the animals and the birds disappeared? Distraction is not something objective, not there outside you; it is something in you. If you cannot accept, you will be distracted; if you accept, distraction disappears.

Once it happened: I was staying in a rest-house. And a political leader was also staying there—a very small rest-house in a very small village. The political leader came to me in the middle of the night, and said, "It is impossible to sleep. How are you sleeping?" He shook me, and said, "How are you sleeping, there is so much distraction?"

Somehow or other at least two dozen dogs . . . they must

have made the rest-house their abode—the whole village's dogs. Maybe they were having a political gathering also—and they were so many; there was such a loud barking and fighting.

He said, "But how are you sleeping? These dogs won't allow me to sleep, and I am tired."

So I said to the political leader, "But they are not aware of you. They don't read newspapers, they don't listen to the radio, they don't look at television; they are not aware of you. I was also here before you. That is their usual way: they are not doing it specially for you. You are fighting, resisting. The notion that they are disturbing you is disturbing you; not they. Accept them." I told him to do one small meditation. "Lie down on the bed. Enjoy their barking. Let it be a music. Enjoy it. Listen to it, as attentively as possible."

He said, "How is it going to help me? I want to avoid, I want to forget that they are there, and you are telling me to listen to them. That will disturb me even more."

I told him, "You just try. You have been trying your way, and it has failed. Now try my way; and you can see that it has been successful with me."

He was not ready for it, and he didn't believe it; but there was no other way, so he tried. And within five minutes he was fast asleep, and snoring. So I went and shook him up, and I said, "How are you sleeping? How is it possible?"

If you accept, nothing can distract you. It is the very rejection in you that creates the distraction. So, if you want to meditate without distraction, don't reject anything. The traffic noise has to be accepted—it is part of this world, and perfectly okay; the child crying and weeping is part of this world, and perfectly okay. Once you say that everything is okay, just watch the feeling that everything is okay and accept it. Something within you melts. Then nothing distracts. And unless this happens, you can go anywhere you like and you will be distracted by one thing or another.

As I understand, most yoga masters teach that withdrawal from the world is necessary. It is not necessary at all. Not only is it not necessary, it is harmful—because who is withdrawing? In withdrawal, the ego will be strengthened. Don't withdraw; rather, melt. I teach you just the opposite. Melt.

Most yoga masters teach that withdrawal from the world is necessary for a period of time, once kundalini *starts rising, until one is finally established in* samadhi; *at which time one can really be in the world, but not of it.* No . . . if you have not been that way from the very beginning, it is not going to happen suddenly in the end. If it has been that way from the very beginning only then will it flower in the end. If you withdraw from the world, you will never be capable of coming back to the world, and being in the world and not of it. No; because it cannot happen suddenly; it is a gradual process. By and by you have to imbibe the spirit of it. It is just like a small seed sprouting, becoming a plant, and becoming a tree. You say that suddenly—first, we will withdraw from the world, and then we will come back to the world. In the very withdrawal you will be disconnected from the world; you will become afraid to come back.

Go and look at Catholic monasteries, Hindu monasteries: people have become afraid; they don't come back. There are monasteries in Europe where, once you enter, you never get out of the monastery again until you die. Why do these monasteries exist? There are monasteries where never in their history has any woman entered . . . Catholic monks. There are monasteries of nuns where no man has ever entered—for centuries. What type of crystallisation is this? Fear crystallised, nothing else— withdrawal crystallised. And they all go on saying that one should live in the world and be not of it. But that has not happened. Look at the Jain monks: they are afraid of everything. For fifty years a man has been a monk—he cannot touch a woman's hand; he cannot look at a woman eye to eye. What type of *samadhi* is this? Maybe suicide, but not *samadhi*. What type of attainment is this? I cannot call it any attainment. It is not that *kundalini* has arisen: *kundalini* has slept completely, died completely. The fire has disappeared. There is no fire.

If you really want to come to that beautiful space where you are in the world and not of it, then you have to be that way from the very beginning; you have to remain in the world and work it out. It is difficult, I know. That's why people escape to the forest, because that looked simple. You think those who have escaped from the world are very brave? Then you are in a totally wrong notion. They are cowards. They have escaped because they could not cope; they have escaped because they could not grow; they have escaped because the world was too much for them. But they have decorated their escape beautifully; and for centuries those cowards have been writing scriptures and commentaries, because they had nothing else to do; and they go on doing that. Their whole energy has been wasted in verbalisation; and they go on convincing other cowards.

Religion is courage; it is not cowardice. Be brave in facing the world. And whatsoever you want to be in the end, be from the very beginning: that is the only way. Carry it from the very first step, because the first step is the last step also.

Your teaching seems to be different: to engage in the world while the transformation is occurring. If this is so, how do I avoid the distraction of maya before I clearly see the reality? There is no need to avoid anything. All effort to avoid is out of fear. Live it; don't avoid it. Live the *maya,* and you will come to know reality, because this *maya* is also a hidden reality. The appearance is also of the reality. Let me repeat it: the appearance is also of the reality. Don't avoid it; otherwise reality will be avoided in it. Go deeply into it. Live it, enjoy it, penetrate it. Hindus have called *maya* the shroud of Brahma, his clothing: don't avoid it. If you avoid my clothes and escape, you will be escaping from me also. You will have to accept my clothes, you will have to come closer and closer; only then can you know me, who is hidden in the clothes.

God is hidden in his *maya*. *Maya* means his magic. God is hidden in his magic. The word 'magic' comes from *maya*. God is hidden in these flowers, in these trees, in these rocks; in you, in me. From every eye he is looking out, from every flower it is his fragrance that is coming out. This is the way he is; this is his appearance. Avoid it, and you will avoid him; enter into it, enter into the fragrance of the flower, and you will find the fragrance of God hidden. Enter any human being in deep love, compassion, humbleness, and behind the body you will find him embodied, and behind the eyes you will find him looking at you. Look into somebody's eyes with deep compassion and love, with deep enquiry, with no prejudice and no idea. Just enter into somebody's eyes, and go deeper and deeper and deeper; and suddenly he is there, in his absolute beauty and purity.

I don't say avoid; that word is dirty for me. I say enter. The *maya* is the temple of God. Enter into it: the world is the temple of God. The body is the temple of God: enter into it. Find as many ways as you can find to enter into it. Try to find God from everywhere and through everything, and you will find him everywhere and in everything. Says Jesus, "Underneath every stone I am hidden. Dig the rock up and you will find me there. Break wood and you will find me there." Everywhere he is. He is the very existence itself, the very is-ness.

Don't try to avoid. Escape, avoid, renunciation, isolation, are wrong words: don't use them. Let them not be part of the vocabulary, your vocabulary; drop them out. Find out positive terms, find out positive words: involvement, commitment, enjoyment, celebration, delight, ecstasy—and you will be on the right path.

The reality and the illusion are not opposites. The God and

his world are not opposites. The God is hidden in the world, and the reality is hiding behind the appearance; and the appearance is also beautiful.

The appearance is also beautiful. Not only is the soul beautiful, the body also is beautiful. And it has to be so, because the soul is hidden behind it. The soul goes on being expressed from the body in millions of ways. The body is just like a glass. Behind it is the flame, and the flame goes on spreading its rays outside the glass. Whenever you see a beautiful person, it simply hints, it simply gives you an indication, that behind it there is some unknown beauty hiding. That's why a beautiful body attracts—it is natural; a beautiful flower attracts—it is natural; because it is simply an indication, a natural indication, an invitation, that something beautiful is hidden behind. Come, investigate me. Come. The beautiful body attracts because of the beautiful soul: you attain to a beautiful body if you attain to a beautiful soul— it is not just coincidence; it is not chance. The more beautiful you become inside, the more beautiful you become on the outside also. If a very ugly body becomes more and more deeply involved in meditation, you will suddenly see the ugliness changing, and behind the ugliness, beauty being expressed more and more. Once the innermost core becomes beautiful, the outer periphery follows it.

The appearance is also beautiful. It happened: a Zen master died, and his chief disciple started crying and weeping. A million people had gathered: the master was very famous; and the chief disciple was even more famous than the master. And those who were closest came to the chief disciple and said, "Please don't cry and weep, because that will create a bad name for you; because people think that you have become a realized soul, and you have been saying yourself that there is no death. Then why are you crying? And you yourself have been teaching your whole life that only the body dies, not the soul. Then why are you crying?"

The chief disciple said, "Yes, I have been telling you that the soul never dies, only the body dies. But who told you that I am crying for the soul? I am crying for the body, because my master's body was so beautiful, and it happens rarely in centuries. Such a beautiful flower surrounded him, because he was so beautiful within. I am crying for the body—who told you that I am crying for the soul? The soul never dies; there is no need to cry for it. But my master's body was also tremendously beautiful, and I will miss it."

This is what I call enlightenment.

My enlightenment is paradoxical. It has to be so, because it is not logical. It is bigger than logic. That's why I go on teaching meditation and love together. Love is part of the *maya,* of the appearance; meditation is part of reality, of God. I go on teaching both. I say, "Love," so that you can penetrate a body deeply, so that you can become aware of the soul which is hidden behind it. And, "Meditate," so that you can attain to your own innermost soul. And let both be together: don't create any dichotomy between the two. It has always been a dichotomy. People who have been teaching meditation have always been against love; and poets and artists, who have been teaching love, have always been against meditation.

I bring the greatest synthesis that is possible in the world to you, the synthesis of love and meditation. And I teach you to grow in both ways. Move in both dimensions: move inwards through meditation, move outwards through love. Go deeper inside yourself, and go farther and farther to the other shore also —so that you don't become lopsided.

Meditators who don't love become lopsided. Their inner being becomes rich, but their outer being becomes very poor. Lovers who are not also meditators—their outer being becomes richer, but their inner being becomes very poor. I would like you to become richer in both ways: love, and meditate.

Bhagwan: you are the only man, if I can call you man, whom I have loved without reservation. With other men I have always wanted to challenge, or overcome. But I had to surrender to you without even offering a token resistance. Now, through your love, you are introducing me to Jesus for the really first time. My deep gratitude for this grace.

Is it easier, at least in the beginning, for women—as potential mothers and lovers—to come to Jesus? Does man come to him through his feminine?

This is from Paritosh. I have initiated many thousands of people on the path, but persons like Paritosh are rare. He is an old man, but you cannot find a more childlike person: it would be difficult. Even little Siddhartha is older than Paritosh. Paritosh is simply innocent: even little Siddhartha is cunning and clever. When little Siddhartha comes to me, he comes like a grown-up man, defensive; but when Paritosh comes to me, he comes like a small child, totally vulnerable, shy like a small child.

On eleventh December, thousands of people passed in front of me, but nobody like Paritosh. He could not even look at me directly: that is too aggressive. He just looked at me out of the side of his eyes, and passed on—a small child—a rare phenomenon. That's what Jesus called, "Unless you become like small children, you will not enter into the kingdom of God." Yes, unless you become like Paritosh, you will not enter into the kingdom of God.

This is his question: *Bhagwan: you are the only man, if I can call you man* ... yes, you can call me man, son of man, just as Jesus calls himself. But I am plus also—son of man and son of God. You are also the same; only your other shore is still unrecognised by you, the other shore is still hidden in the morning mist. You have not come to see your own height. You have lived in the porch of your life; you have not entered the palace. The porch is not all: you are more than yourself, you are greater than yourself, you are higher than yourself, you are deeper than yourself. That which is higher than yourself, deeper than yourself, is what we call **God.**

You are just like me—there is not a bit of difference. You are just like Jesus—there is no difference at all. But Jesus has recognised his other shore, Jesus has recognised that he is more than himself. Hence he calls himself son of God and son of man, both.

You can call me man; but Paritosh is hesitant, because he can see, at least he can feel, that something more is also there. He says: *You are the only man, if I can call you man* ... because he feels something more also. Grow into that feeling. And that should not be about me only; by and by let it be about yourself also. Then you will not only love yourself, you will even revere yourself, you will also respect. Just the other day I was telling you: love yourself. Now I tell you: worship also. If you love yourself you become man, rightly a human being; if you worship yourself also, which is tremendously difficult but not impossible, then you become God also. When the worshipper and the worshipped are one, then God has happened to you. Then you need not go to any temple; then the temple has come to you.

You are the only man, if I can call you man, whom I have loved without reservation. I know it. From the very first day Paritosh came, his surrender has been total.

With other men I have always wanted to challenge, or overcome. But I had to surrender to you without even offering token resistance.

Why has it happened? Because if you can see me, then I am not other than you; then there is no point in giving resistance, then there is no point in struggling, then you will be struggling against yourself. When you surrender to me, what is happening actually is this: that your lower self is surrendering to your own higher self. I am just an excuse.

Now, through your love, you are introducing me to Jesus for the really first time. Jesus has been taught from a thousand and one pulpits; his name has been used for these two thousand years as nobody else's name has ever been used. More books are written on Jesus than on anybody else. More churches stand in his name than in anybody else's name. Millions of preachers all around the world, millions of missionaries, go on propagating his name and his word; and I tell you, Jesus is one of the very unknown masters. In fact, the very dust that missionaries have raised around his name, the very smoke that theology has created, has become a barrier in understanding him. The moment the name Jesus is uttered, immediately the Vatican, the pope, the church and the whole establishment, come to mind. And whatsoever they have been doing in the name of Jesus has been simply ugly, horrible— it has been a nightmare.

That's why, when I talk about Jesus, you feel I am bringing a new breeze to you—because I am not a missionary, I am not a Christian, I am not a priest. In fact I have nothing to do with Jesus, except that I love him. When I bring Jesus to you, I am bringing myself; through his name, through his word, I am expressing myself. It is not Jesus and me, as two; it is one phenomenon. Sometimes it is almost impossible to say whether I am speaking on Jesus or Jesus himself is speaking on himself. Sometimes the boundaries completely merge.

Those moments come when you are listening from your heart. Then boundaries completely merge; then I disappear. Then Jesus talks through me; then I can become a vehicle. Because I have no prejudice for or against, and I have no dogma to preach, Jesus can come in his crystal purity to you.

Is it easier, at least in the beginning, for women—as potential mothers and lovers—to come to Jesus? Does man come to him through his feminine? Yes. In fact, God comes to you always through your feminine part—because the feminine part means the receptivity, your receptivity. You cannot be aggressive towards God, you cannot possess him, you cannot attack and take him over: you can only allow, in deep humbleness, in deep receptivity— you open. Just as a flower opens to the sun, you open to the divine. You cannot do anything about it, because your doing will be from your male part. Every man is half-man and half-woman; every woman is half-woman and half-man. The difference is not much. A man's man-part, male part, is on top, and the feminine part below. In man, the man is conscious and the woman is unconscious; in woman, the woman is conscious and the man unconscious.

Of course it is true, absolutely true, that whenever a man like Jesus walks the earth, or a Buddha, or a Mahavir, then women are attracted first—because they can receive immediately: their conscious part is feminine. Mary Magdalene is closer to Jesus than any Peter; it has to be so, because she is not an intellect, she is a heart. She loves him, and love is always total. When men come to Jesus, they need to be convinced, they need to be convinced intellectually. When a woman comes, she needs only one conviction: the conviction of the heart. And the heart has its own reasons that reason knows not. It simply falls in love; it trusts.

So Jesus or Buddha are easily understood by women; they come immediately and easily close to them, because they can be open naturally. Their whole biology is of receptivity. They have a passivity—they can open; they are not aggressive, and they can open and allow. And Jesus can enter into them.

For man it is difficult in the beginning, because he has to fight, to struggle; he has to be intellectually convinced. There is

going to be a war. Unless he is defeated, unless he has tried all
ways by which he could escape, he will not surrender. His surrender is only in the end. Once he surrenders, then his feminine
part starts functioning.

It is easy for women in the beginning; it is difficult for men
in the beginning. But one thing more has to be understood: it
is difficult for women in the end, and easier for men in the end.
Because the deeper the love goes, the more woman passes from
her feminine to her male part. You must have watched: you
fall in love with a woman; she is so nice in the beginning. And
there is no need to talk about the end—how nasty a woman can
become! When the male part comes up, she starts becoming
nasty, starts fighting, quarrelling—every woman. In the beginning she is just honey, not of this world; in the end, very
poisonous.

So it is easier for a woman to come closer to me, or to Jesus,
in the beginning. It is difficult for men in the beginning: they
will have to fight. But in the end the whole process reverses: the
woman starts fighting, and the man starts surrendering.

So they are equal on the whole. But if you are aware, if a
man is aware, there is no need to fight in the beginning—from
the very beginning he can become open, as Paritosh has been
from the very beginning. And if a woman is aware, there is no
need to fight in the end. She can remain open. But for that,
awareness will be needed. If you move unaware, then you are
just victims of your own conscious and unconscious minds.
Awareness leads you beyond; then you can use your conscious
and unconscious minds, but you are not used by them.

So, those who have feminine bodies and feminine minds
should be alert. They should not be satisfied from the beginning;
and they should not feel contented that they have come close
to me—their real problem is going to arise later on. But if they
remain aware, the problem need not arise: there is no necessity
for it. The necessity exists in your unawareness. If you remain

aware, you can pass through that barrier. And, if you are aware from the very beginning, and you have a male body and mind, the awareness will be enough: you need not fight, because fight leads nowhere.

A deep rapport is needed, not fight. And it is not a question of intellectual conviction. A conversion is needed, not conviction. And conversion comes when you are in rapport with me. When you feel me, live me; when you allow me to go deepest in you, and you are not afraid, then conversion happens. And conversion is needed—conviction won't help.

So, if you are men, be alert from the very beginning. If you are women, then be alert: sooner or later the male part of you will arise. Both have to be alert.

Awareness is neither male nor female, because it does not belong to the body; it hovers above the body. People come to me and ask, "Where is the location of awareness?" It cannot be located, because it is not part of the body. It hovers somewhere above you. It is not exactly in the body; it cannot be located. And once you become aware, you also hover over your body: you are not in the body. That is the meaning of the English word 'ecstasy'. Ecstasy means standing out of oneself, ecstasy: standing out.

When you become aware, you become ecstatic: you stand outside yourself. You become a watcher on the hills.

JOHN 7

25 Then said some of them of Jerusalem . . .

27 Howbeit we know this man whence he is:
    but when Christ cometh,
    no man knoweth whence he is.

28 Then cried Jesus in the temple
    as he taught, saying,
    Ye both know me, and ye know whence I am:
    and I am not come of myself,
    but he that sent me is true,
    whom ye know not.

29 But I know him:
    for I am from him,
    and he hath sent me.

30 Then they sought to take him:
    but no man laid hands on him,
    because his hour was not yet come.

31   And many of the people believed on him,
     and said,
     When Christ cometh,
     will he do more miracles than these
     which this man hath done?

32   The Pharisees heard that the people
     murmured such things concerning him;
     and the Pharisees and the chief priests
     sent officers to take him.

33   Then said Jesus unto them,
     Yet a little while am I with you,
     and then I go unto him that sent me . . .

37   In the last day,
     that great day of the feast,
     Jesus stood and cried, saying,
     If any man thirst,
     let him come unto me, and drink.

9 *Jesus is water of eternity, a divine well. He can quench your thirst.*

HE OTHER day I was reading a few lines from e.e. cummings:

> seeker of truth
> follow no path
> all paths lead where
> truth is here.

Truth is always here. That's the only way truth can be. Truth cannot be anywhere else. The only time it can be is here, and the only place it can be is now. But the mind is never here and is never now. Hence, mind and truth never meet.

The mind goes on thinking about truth, and the truth goes on waiting to be realized, but the meeting never happens. The meeting is possible only if mind stops functioning, because mind means the past, mind means the future. Mind is never herenow. Whenever you start thinking, you are going astray. If you stop thinking, suddenly you are at home. You had never gone from there; the whole wandering is like a dream. Otherwise, you have lived in God, you have lived as gods—that's the only way to be. But you don't realize it, because you go on thinking about it.

The rose is before your eyes, but you are too full of ideas about the rose. Jesus was standing right there and people were thinking —and he was in front of them. But they were not there; they were thinking about the scriptures, what the scriptures say.

Then said some of them of Jerusalem . . .

It is meaningful that the gospel says, "Some of the people who said these words belonged to Jerusalem"—the sacred place, the holy place. The holy place becomes the most unholy, because when people think they know, they are the most unholy. When people think they know, they are the most ignorant people, because those who know, know that they know not. It has happened always. Go to Varanasi and you will find only parrots—great scholars, but without any realization. Go to Mecca, and you will find *maulwis* who know everything about, and know nothing; who can recite the whole Koran—they have memorized it. They have become great computers, but the knowledge of reality has not dawned on them. Their innermost shrine remains dark, unlit, and they go on talking about light.

It is meaningful that the gospel says:

Then said some of them of Jerusalem . . .

Jerusalem is the Mecca of the Jews. Then it became the Mecca of Christians also. It is the Varanasi of the West. Whenever a certain place becomes a sacred place, it loses all sacredness— otherwise, the whole existence is holy. But whenever religion is organized, truth made a doctrine, scholars becoming more important than mystics, information becoming more important than knowledge, then this misfortune happens.

Those people of Jerusalem—they knew all. "When Jesus comes," the scriptures say, "nobody will know from where he comes."

> *Howbeit we know this man whence he is:*
> they said,
> *but when Christ cometh,*
> *no man knoweth whence he is.*

A very pertinent question—because they knew it well—from where this man comes. They knew his father, his mother, brothers and sisters; they knew all about them. And this information clouded their minds. In fact, do you know from where you come? Do you come from your father? Do you come from your mother? Maybe you come through them, but you don't come from them. Maybe you pass through them. They may be like crossroads, but you don't come out of them.

It is said when Buddha became enlightened and came back to visit his father, the father was very angry and said, "I can forgive you because I have a father's heart. But drop all this nonsense. You belong to the family of an emperor. Don't move like a beggar. You are my son."

Buddha laughed and said, "Sir, I may come through you, but I don't belong to you. I may come through you, but I don't belong to you. To whom do *you* belong?"

If you go deeper into yourself, you will find a mysterious silence. No answer comes. Your body may have been contributed by your mother and father, but not your consciousness. Your mind may even have been contributed by the society, by the community, by your family, by the education—but not your consciousness. That one who you are comes from nowhere.

Yes, the scriptures say and they say rightly:

> *. . . when Christ cometh,*
> *no man knoweth whence he is.*

I tell you, the moment you come to know that you know not from where you are, you have become a Christ. This is the whole meaning of it. The moment you realize that your origin is shrouded in mystery, that your beginning and your end are mysterious, and there is no way to know them because you have been always and always and always. . . . In fact there has never been a beginning—that's the meaning, when I say they are shrouded in mystery. They cannot be known, because there has been no beginning to know.

You have been here before time started: you have been here before space ever existed. And you will be here to the very end of time, and even after that. Time came after you, so there is no beginning.

Once you realize this, suddenly you have become the Christ. The realization that 'I am beyond time', is the meaning of the word 'Christ'. The scriptures say it perfectly and rightly, but when parrots recite scriptures the whole meaning is lost. Not only have they not understood what is said, they have also misunderstood.

Christ is standing before them: a man who has realized that he comes from nowhere. God means 'nowhere', God means 'no when', God means 'the source, which is beyond beginning and beyond end'. The source has to be beyond beginning and beyond end.

It happened once: Diogenes put up a tent in the marketplace, in Athens, on a very busy crossroad. On the tent he wrote "Wisdom sold here."

One of the richest men was passing and looked at it. He laughed and he told his servant to go with five gold coins and ask this braggard, "How much wisdom can you give for five gold coins?"

The servant went while the rich man waited outside. Diogenes pocketed the money, and wrote a small wisdom-bit on a piece of paper, and gave it to the servant. It said, "Whatsoever you do, always remember your beginning and your end."

The rich man had laughed before, but now he became serious. And he loved that wisdom-bit so much that he had it written on his palace in gold letters: "Whatsoever you do, always remember your beginning and your end."

Whatsoever you do is meaningless, unless somehow it is related to your beginning and your end. If you go on doing things which are not related to your beginning and to your end—that means if they are not related to God—then your life will be trivia, a heap of rubbish: it won't carry any meaning. Meaning belongs to the whole, meaning belongs to the source and the culmination.

If you forget the source and the end, your life will be just a drifting thing—meaningless coincidences. There will not be a running theme in it, and there will not be significance in it. You will not really exist; you will just live. You may continue living, but your life will not have a rhythm, it will not be a song, it will not have inner consistency, it will not be relevant.

Howbeit we know this man whence he is:

Nobody knows. You don't even know from where you come. But those people thought they knew well.

> *. . . from whence he is:*
> *but when Christ cometh,*
> *no man knoweth whence he is.*

The scriptures speak absolute truth, but nobody knows from where anybody comes. The source is mysterious; it is shrouded. And there is no way to know it, because you are the knower and you can never become the known. Let me repeat it: you are the knower and you can never be reduced to be the known. You are the subjectivity and you can never become the object. So how can you know yourself, who you are? How can you know yourself, from where you come? How can you know the beginning?

This feeling that I don't know who I am, this feeling that I don't know from where I come, this feeling that I don't know where I'm going—if it becomes intense, the ego drops. Because then there are no props for it—then the ego cannot stand.

The ego needs three props. It is a three-legged stool: who am I?—from where do I come?—where am I going? These three legs are needed for the ego. If these three legs disappear, the ego falls.

Once it happened: One of the greatest rich men of this century, Andrew Carnegie, was asked by a man, "What do you think, sir, is the most important thing in industry—money, labour or banks?" Andrew Carnegie said, "It is a three-legged stool."

And which leg is more important? In fact, if you withdraw one leg, the stool will fall. The two legs won't be able to help it. If you withdraw one thing, if you start feeling, "I don't know who I am," immediately the other two legs will be useless. Or, if you withdraw the first leg, "I don't know from where I come," then the other two will not be of any use. The props will drop and the ego will fall. Ego is a three-legged stool.

You have at least to believe who you are—your name, your form; from where you have come—your family; where you are going—a certain idea about your destiny: then the ego can exist.

A man becomes a Christ when all these three legs disappear. That's why the old scriptures say:

> ... *when Christ cometh,*
> *no man knoweth whence he is* ...

And Christ was standing before these blind people, and they were asking foolish questions and arguing about foolish things. And they were very clever people, the people of Jerusalem. They were very intelligent, clever people; they could argue and discuss. In fact, Jesus was not so educated, so well-informed, as they were. Jesus was an uneducated man—in a sense, uncultured, unsophisticated. And remember, God has happened many more times to unsophisticated people than to sophisticated people, because the sophisticated person believes that he already knows. Once you think that you know, then there is no possibility of knowing.

I will tell you a story. Once a prospector climbed a mountain to seek for gold. On the way up, he fell down and struck his head. In his dizziness, he imagined he had found hundreds of gold nuggets. So, wandering around town, he offered nonexistent gold to everyone he met. Of course, he had become mad, and had become the laughing stock of the whole community.

A sage took pity on him—on the poor rich man. He hit him hard on the head. The blow cleared his head. In shock and dismay he realized his former folly. "How incredible of me to imagine I possessed gold," he told himself.

Then an astonishing thing happened. Once he realized that he didn't possess gold, he began to search, and to find gold nuggets. Once realizing he didn't possess gold, he started to search. And when you seek, you find.

Spiritual riches follow awareness of poverty. That is the one and the only order of things. Says Buddha, "*Aes dhammo sanantano.*" This is the eternal law, that once you realize you are spiritually poor, you are already on the way to being rich. Once you realize that you are ignorant, you have taken the first and the most basic step towards wisdom. Once you realize that you have gone astray, your life is already changing. Now the true path is not far away.

But if you think that you are not astray, that you are on the right path, that you know, that you already possess that which you don't possess, then there is no possibility. Then you are closed.

Anyone can see the difference between real and imaginary riches. He can enquire. You can enquire—and always enquire! Let this be a criterion to find out whether your riches are imaginary or real: "Do I feel rich when all by myself, or do I constantly need others to reassure me?" Go on asking this question. If you can feel rich when just by yourself, alone—and you don't need anybody else to reassure you, you don't need anybody else's opinion, anybody else's certificate that you are rich—if you can be rich when all by yourself, then your riches are real. If you need constant reassurance from others, then your riches are unreal, imaginary. Then you are just depending on others' opinions. Remember this.

Many times people come to me to be reassured. They ask, they say, "I'm feeling very happy and blissful. What do you say?" What is the need to say anything? The very need shows that the happiness is unreal and imaginary.

If you are really feeling happy, you are feeling happy even if the whole world contradicts you. If the whole world agrees that you are not happy, then too it doesn't matter. Your happiness is real. It cannot be cancelled by anybody's opinion. But if your happiness is unreal, it can be cancelled by anybody. Even a small child can cancel it. You will be constantly looking towards people. You will be smiling, trying to show that you are happy so that they can say, "Yes. You are very happy. You look very happy."

Always remember this criterion: only the false needs support; the real is self-evident. Only the false needs certificates; the real is self-evident.

People used to ask Christ, "From where is your authority?" —the authority is *his*.

It happened: When I came out of the university, I applied for a government job. The education minister called me for an interview and asked for some character certificates.

I said, "I am here; you look at me. I can sit here; you can

watch me. I can live with you for a few days if you like. But don't ask about certificates. Who can give me a character certificate?"

He couldn't understand. He said, "You can bring one from your vice-chancellor, or at least from the head of your department."

I said, "If my vice-chancellor asks for a character certificate from me, I am not going to give it to him. So how can I ask for a character certificate from him? I cannot give one to him. So that is impossible. I can ask for a character certificate only from a man whom I can see is a man of character. But that will be absurd. That means that first I give him a character certificate—only then his character certificate becomes meaningful."

But he couldn't follow me. He said, "Then it will be difficult, because at least two character certificates are needed."

So I wrote a character certificate in the name of my vice-chancellor. And I went to the vice-chancellor later on and said, "I have given in the true copy, the original I don't have. This is the certificate I have given to myself. You have to sign it."

He said, "But this is absurd." He said, "How can you give a character certificate to yourself?"

I told him, "If I cannot give one to myself, then who can give one to me? I know myself more than anybody else knows me. You don't know me at all. If you can give a character certificate to me, then why can't I? This is the certificate. You have to sign it."

He looked at the certificate and laughed, because I had written on the certificate that man is a freedom, and character is always of the past, and the future remains open. I may have been a good man up to now. Next moment? Nobody knows! I may have been a saint up to now, but the next moment I can become a sinner. In fact, each moment I have to give a new lease to my character; again and again and again I have to hold it.

Character belongs to the past, and you ask for a character

certificate to be reassured about the future—which is foolish.
The future remains open; the future remains always open. Next
moment is always indeterminate. That's the difference between
a stone and a man. You can give a character certificate to a rock.
The rock is consistent; it has always remained a rock, and it is
always going to remain a rock. It is predictable. But how can
you give a character certificate to a man?

A sinner sometimes becomes a saint, a saint becomes a sinner.
That is the beauty of man: that man has no character. Only
rocks have character. The more alive you are, the less character
—absolutely alive, no character. Then you are absolute freedom.

Facing Christ, people ask about authority; they ask about
character. They ask that Christ should fulfil the predictions of
the scriptures. Why should Christ fulfil the predictions of the
scriptures? He is not a rock. He is total freedom, absolute freedom—that is his beauty and glory. But people believe in dead
things, people believe in dead gods. They are dead; they feel
comfortable with dead gods. If you are alive, only then can you
feel comfortable with an alive God. An alive God means freedom.

Each moment one has to decide again and again who one is
going to be; each moment is a decisive moment, and each moment
you can change everything. You may not change; that too is
your decision. But each moment one has to decide continuously,
constantly. Character is not something which is there just like
a dead rock. It has to be lived, acted, decided. Each moment you
are born again and again. Each moment you die, and each
moment you are born again and again.

But people go on asking. And the people of Jerusalem or
Varanasi—they are the deadest people there are. Jerusalem is
one of the most ancient cities in the world. That means it carries
a very long and dead past, and always thinks in terms of the past,
never in terms of the future. They couldn't see the future.
The Jews missed Christ.

With Christ was the destiny and the future; but they were

asking questions about the past. They couldn't see; they had no
eyes to perceive that a new beginning had started. God had taken
a new step in this man, God had taken a new decision in this
man. God had taken a very decisive and historical decision. The
whole humanity would be different through this man. Man will
no more be the same as he was before—a turning point. But
that is all in the future.

The Jews were standing there. Jesus was an opening towards
the future, but they were looking at the past. They were looking
at the clouds of dust that were left behind. They couldn't see
the sun that was rising.

> *Howbeit we know this man whence he is:*
> *but when Christ cometh,*
> *no man knoweth whence he is.*

> *Then cried Jesus in the temple*
> *as he taught, saying,*
> *Ye both know me, and ye know whence I am:*
> *And I am not come of myself,*
> *but he that sent me is true,*
> *whom ye know not.*

Jesus cried. People like Jesus have to cry, because we are
deaf. And even when they cry, we don't listen. And even when
we listen, we don't understand. And even when we understand, we don't act.

I will tell you one story: A group of unhappy men and women
heard about a peaceful place called the Celestial City. Wishing
to live in it, they consulted a wise man who told them: "Go to
the edge of the town. There you will see footprints. Follow them
all the way to the Celestial City."

When locating the footprints, part of the group turned back

immediately, complaining, "But they lead straight into the
frightening wilderness."

The rest of the group followed the footprints for a short
distance, but several more stopped when it started to rain. After
a few more miles, the group broke up into two quarrelling
factions, each demanding the right to lead the expedition. The
battle raged so fiercely that they forgot all about the Celestial
City, and returned home to continue the fight.

When observing all this, the wise man explained to his
disciples: "Because of man's dazed mind, this is what always
happens. Still, people must be told about the footprints. Every
once in a while, a perservering man or woman follows them all
the way to the Celestial City."

Man goes on misunderstanding. God goes on sending his
messengers; man goes on misinterpreting. God goes on making
new efforts; man goes on crucifying. God goes on hoping,
God hopes tremendously. He is not yet frustrated with you.
He still hopes; his hope is eternal. Whatsoever you do makes no
difference to his hope. He goes on making new efforts, he goes
on devising new methods.

A Jesus is a device, a Buddha is a device, a Krishna is a device.
God comes again and again in different forms. Maybe you re-
jected one form; you may accept another. He hopes continuously.
Remember this.

And always remember that I'm not talking about those
people who sometime lived in Jerusalem; I am talking about you.
I am not talking about some fools who couldn't understand
Jesus; I am talking about you—because it is always the same.
Always Jesus is there and always people are quarrelling about
meaningless doctrines and dogmas—quoting scriptures, creating
smoke around themselves and not looking at the fact.

Jesus is a divine fact. God is standing in front of them and
they are asking whether he is really the God. What was the
trouble that they could not believe in him?—because Jesus could

not follow all the predictions of the old prophets. Nobody is there to follow anybody else's predictions. And this is the foolishness: Jews rejected Christ because they thought he didn't follow all the predictions; Christians go on proving that he followed all the predictions. That's why they accept him.

Look at the foolishness—it is the same. Nobody looks at Jesus directly. Jews reject him, but the argument is the same: that he does not follow all the predictions that the scriptures say a Christ has to follow. Christians say that he does follow them. The argument is the same; the mind is the same. They don't differ. Both are missing. They may be standing opposite each other, but their attitude is the same. Nobody is looking at Christ; nobody is following the footprints to the Celestial City. They have come back home to continue the fight.

> *Then cried Jesus in the temple*
> *as he taught, saying,*
> *Ye both know me, and ye know whence I am:*

He is saying, "You know not; you don't know me. You don't know whence I am, and I am not come of myself."

Nobody has come that way. Everybody comes from God. In fact, nobody comes, everybody is sent. Everybody comes from the whole. Were you asked to decide whether you would like to come to the world or not? Nobody has ever asked. It has never been your decision. You have been sent; the whole has sent you. As the ocean waves itself into thousands and thousands of waves, so God waves in humanity, in life, in thousands and thousands of waves. You are a wave in his consciousness. You may have started to feel that you are separate, but that is illusion, that is *maya*.

> *And I am not come of myself,*
> *but he that sent me is true,*
> *whom ye know not.*

Jesus is not saying anything about the man Jesus. He is talking about each human consciousness. Whatsoever he's saying about himself is relevant to you also. There, again, Jews thought that he was very egoistic: he claims that he comes from God—and a prophet has to be humble. He doesn't seem to be humble at all. Christians think that he is claiming something about himself, not about everybody else.

So if somebody else says, "I am the son of God," Christians will be immediately against him. "This man is a heretic. There has been one, and only one, son of God, and that's Jesus Christ, the only begotten son."

What I am trying to show you is that the mind is the same—whether it is Jewish or Christian makes no difference. Mind as such is stupid, and unless the mind is dropped you can become a Jew or a Christian or a Hindu; it is not going to make any difference.

> *But I know him:*
> *for I am from him,*
> *and he hath sent me.*

This is beautiful, the word 'sent'. Nobody comes; everybody is sent. Everybody is a messenger because everybody carries a message within himself, a destiny to be fulfilled, a seed. You are not from yourself. Nobody is, nobody can be. Everybody comes out of the whole and the whole must be sending a coded message in you. You may not have deciphered it yet, you may not have been able to decode it yet. One who decodes it understands. Jesus decoded it. He understood the message—why he had been sent.

The first thing to realize very deeply is that you have not come—you have been sent. Small words make a lot of difference.

I have heard about a warrior in Japan. In the First World War, he was a samurai, a great warrior. One arm was hurt very much, wounded very much—it had to be removed. After the operation, when the warrior came back to consciousness, the surgeon told him, "I am very sorry that you had to lose your arm."

The warrior tried to raise himself up and protested. He said, "I have not lost it; I gave it."

"I have not lost it; I gave it"—tremendously different. He has given it.

If you say Jesus lost his life, you will be wrong. He gave it, he gave it for us. He gave it for the message, he gave it for the mission for which he was sent.

> *. . . for I am from him,*
> *and he hath sent me.*

Always remember: whenever Jesus talks about God, he means the whole. His terminology is not as perfect as Buddha's. Even Buddha's terminology is not as perfect as Lao Tzu's. Terminology does not depend on Buddha, Jesus, or Lao Tzu; it depends on the people to whom they are talking.

Jesus was talking to Hebrews, to Jews. They have a terminology. He has to use it; there was no other way. If he had started talking like a Buddha, nobody would have understood—not at all. Even when he was using their own terminology, he was not understood. There is no possibility that if he had used the terminology of Buddha, that he would have been understood; because the terminology of Buddha needs a long heritage of Upanishadic teaching. Buddha was against the Upanishads, but the Upanishads prepared the background. Without the Upanishads he could not have been here.

Lao Tzu uses such a beautiful terminology that nobody can ever find a fault with it. But that is the reason he could never become such a great religious leader as Buddha or Jesus: nobody understood him. He talks very simply; he is the simplest possible man. He has no jargon; he does not use the word 'God' at all. He does not use any terminology of theology, religion. Because of this, nobody understood him. Nobody even tried to crucify him; nobody threw even a stone at him, because even for that you have at least to be misunderstood. If you don't understand, okay. But you have at least to misunderstand. Lao Tzu was simply neglected.

I have heard a story. Once he was going from one town to another on his donkey. A messenger from the emperor came and told Lao Tzu, "The emperor has heard about you and he would like you to become a part of his court. He needs wise men there."

Lao Tzu treated the messenger very courteously, but said, "No, it is impossible. I am grateful. Thank the emperor, but it is impossible."

When the messenger was gone, Lao Tzu washed his ears with water, and washed the ears of the donkey also.

A man who was standing by the road asked, "What are you doing, sir?"

He said, "I am washing my ears, because even the message from the world of politics is dangerous."

The man asked, "But why are you washing the ears of the donkey?"

He said, "Donkeys are very political. He is already walking in a different way! The moment he heard and saw the messenger from the court, he became very egoistic. Donkeys tend to be political. I don't much understand the language of the court, but he understands, because similar donkeys are there. The language is the same."

The man laughed. It is said, even when the story was reported to the king, that he also laughed.

People laughed about Lao Tzu; at the most, a crazy old man, eccentric, but nobody took him seriously. And he could never influence people to such an extent that they should organize his teaching. No religion, no organization, could come out of his teachings. He remained alone. He remains alone, but purest.

Jesus was talking to Jews. They have a particular terminology of God—'prophets', 'kingdom of God'. He has to use that. But remember always, whenever he says 'God' he means tao; he cannot mean anything else. Don't ask me by what authority I say this. I am not a pope; I am not a Vatican pope. I have no authority. But I say to you, by my own authority, whenever he says 'God' he means tao. Whenever he says *he hath sent me* he means 'the whole has sent me'. Then Jesus will appear in a different light. Then you will be able to understand him more, and follow him more, and go further than ordinarily you could go with him.

> *Then they sought to take him:*
> *but no man laid hands on him,*
> *because his hour was not yet come.*

Existence is not a chaos, it is a cosmos. Existence is not just by chance. It has a story to tell, it has a running theme, it has a song to sing. It is a great drama; Hindus call it 'leela', a great drama, a great play. That is what is meant by this gospel sentence, this sutra: *because his hour was not yet come.* This is a deep acceptance of things.

The people who wrote the gospel were closest to Jesus. They understood one thing: that whatsoever was happening, was happening as part of a great drama. If you have that feeling, you start accepting things. They could accept even the crucifixion of Jesus, because that was part of the great drama. It was meant to be so. They could accept it, because it was not just chance, not just coincidence—it had to be so.

A Judas has to betray Jesus, because whenever a Jesus is there a shadow falls; just as when you walk in the sun and a shadow follows you. Whenever in the world of consciousness somebody rises so high, a shadow falls; that shadow is the Judas. It has to be so.

And whenever you want to transform humanity, whenever you want to bring a new truth into human consciousness, the human mind defends itself—it becomes aggressive against you. Jesus has to be crucified. That's how the human mind functions. It is a great drama; it is a cosmos. Then everything is accepted. Once you look at life not as unrelated facts, but as a related whole, then everything fits in. Then there is no need to complain; then there is no need to feel frustrated, or to feel that there is injustice.

Just try to see the beauty of it. Jesus was crucified, but the closest disciples never felt that something wrong had happened. Not that they didn't miss him. They missed him, they missed him tremendously. Not that they didn't cry for him. They cried—but they accepted. They accepted, because it must be so. There must be a meaning in it; we may not be able to know the meaning, but there must be a meaning in it—because nothing can happen which is meaningless, nothing can happen which is unrelated to the whole.

We may not be able to know the meaning of a certain fact, because we know only the isolated fact; we cannot see the whole in relation to it. Whatsoever we see is just as if suddenly you have come across a page of a book—a strong wind has just brought a page of a book to your door. Out of curiosity you start reading it; you cannot make any sense out of it because it is just a page. You don't know what happened before; you don't know what happened afterwards.

All the facts that we know are just pages—not even pages, broken sentences—not even broken sentences, broken words. The whole book of existence is so vast, so eternal, we cannot know what it means, because meaning always means relevance concerning the whole, in relationship with the whole.

Poetry is meaningful because you can relate words one with another; they are not unrelated. It is meaningful, because between the words you can see the flow of a certain meaning. If you cannot see the meaning, if you just cut a few words from a dictionary and paste them with closed eyes on paper, and then read it, there will be no meaning—separate words, not connected.

Then they sought to take him:
but no man laid hands on him,
because his hour was not yet come.

And many of the people believed on him,
and said,
When Christ cometh,
will he do more miracles than these
which this man hath done?

Ordinary people believe in miracles—they can't see the phenomenon, the tremendous phenomenon that has happened. They think only of miracles. This man touched somebody and the man was healed; or this man touched somebody else, and the man was blind, and his eyes were restored. These are great miracles for the ordinary mind. Magicians are more impressive. They can't see the only miracle that has happened in this man; the very being of this man is a miracle. All other miracles are just by-products. Not that he is doing them—Jesus never said, "I have done miracles."

Once a woman touched him. She was afraid to come in front of him. She had leprosy and she was ugly. She was afraid to come in front of him and ask to be healed, but she had faith. She just touched him. When Jesus was passing through the crowd, just from behind she touched his body. Suddenly, Jesus turned. The woman was healed, and said, in deep gratefulness, "You healed me, Lord."

Jesus said, "Don't say that. Your faith has healed you."

Your faith—not Jesus. Many times he says, "It is God who has healed you, not me." He is just a vehicle. But people are more interested in miracles. Scholars are interested in scriptures; ordinary people are more interested in miracles. Nobody seems to be interested in the facts of this man who is standing before them, this tremendously innocent energy, this flowering of consciousness. Nobody is interested in looking directly at Jesus.

The Pharisees heard that the people
murmured such things concerning him;
and the Pharisees and the chief priests
sent officers to take him.

These are the three types of people Jesus is surrounded by continuously: the crowd who believe in miracles, the people who have their investments in religion—the priests, the Pharisees, who are afraid that this man is becoming every day more and more important—and the scholars, the pundits, the rabbis, who are interested only in dead scriptures, in dead words, in knowledge. These are the three types of people he is continuously surrounded by.

The fourth type are very few, who are trying to understand who this man is, who are not worried about scriptures, because the scripture is alive herenow. They are not worried about miracles, because the greatest of all miracles has happened: that a man has realized that he is not separate from the whole. The ego has disappeared: that is the greatest miracle there is.

The fourth type are people who have no investment in religion, who have no self-interest in religion, who are not worried about the temple and the establishment and other things—a very few people who are interested just in this man as he is, without any prejudice, without any concept. These few people could see through Jesus and could find God through him. He became a door.

Jesus says again and again, "I am the gate. I am the door. I am the way." Only for a few people he was so, for those whose eyes were not clouded by anything, who could look through this man, through and through.

Then said Jesus unto them,
Yet a little while am I with you,
and then I go unto him that sent me . . . .

It is such a great phenomenon that it cannot be longer. The earth won't allow it.

I was reading the life of one Urdu poet, Miraja Galib. In a poet's gathering, a very young boy, just twelve or thirteen years of age, recited such beautiful poetry of his own creation that Galib, a master, asked the boy again and again to recite it. And in the end, Galib started crying and weeping.

Somebody asked, "Why are you crying?"

Galib said, "This boy will not live long." And just within six months, the boy died.

People asked, "Why do you say this?"

Galib said, "He is so beautiful. He has something tremendous in him. Earth will not be able to tolerate such beauty. He is not ordinary, he is not mediocre."

*W*henever a man becomes enlightened, that is his last life. Then he cannot enter again into the world, because the world is too rough, and he becomes too refined. Then he is just a fragrance, subtle, with no solidity in it, and then the fragrance goes up higher and higher. It cannot come down. Whenever a man becomes enlightened, it is difficult to remain in the body— almost impossible. One has to be continuously aware; any moment, the body can drop.

Jesus continuously says to his disciples, "Yet a little while am I with you, and then I go unto him that sent me . . . and then I return to the whole." Then the wave disappears in the ocean.

In the last day,
that great day of the feast,
Jesus stood and cried, saying,
If any man thirst,
let him come unto me, and drink.

I have heard: The day Woodrow Wilson died, the doctors,

feeling that his death was coming closer and closer, apprised him about the nearness of death. Just a few seconds before he died, they decided to tell the old man. They told him that death was coming closer and closer. He opened his eyes and said, "Ready"—that was all—closed his eyes, a smile on his face, and disappeared.

A Jesus is always ready—readiness to go back, readiness to fall back onto the shores—because a Jesus is ripe. And whenever a fruit is ripe, the fruit can say, "Yet a little while I am with you—with the tree, a little while—and then I go unto him that sent me." And then the fruit drops to the earth, and disappears into the earth from where it came.

Whenever you have become ripe, you disappear. That is the meaning of the Eastern concept of becoming free from birth and death. Whenever you become ready, there is no need for you to be thrown back into existence again and again. You are thrown back because you don't learn the lesson. It is like a child who fails every time and has to be sent back again to the same class. If he learns the lesson, passes the examination, then he is sent to another class, a higher one. And when he finishes his education, then there is no need to go back there. The world is a training, a discipline. You are sent again and again, because you have not yet learned the lesson. Once you learn it, you are back to the original source.

Jesus is constantly aware, Buddha is constantly aware. Whether Buddha lasted for forty years and Jesus lasted only for three years, it doesn't make much difference, because in the vast eternity, forty years is just a little longer.

In the last day,
that great day of the feast,
Jesus stood and cried, saying,
—before he was crucified—
If any man thirst,
let him come unto me, and drink.

". . . because soon I will disappear and then you will not be able to drink from me. If any man thirsts, if somebody is thirsty, let him come and drink of me, because soon I will be gone, and then you can think about me, but you will not be able to quench your thirst."

Jesus is water of eternity, a divine well. He can quench your thirst. But people are not aware even of their thirst. They have forgotten their thirst; they have suppressed it. That's why he says *If any man thirst* . . .

Everybody is thirsty. There is no need to say 'if'. Have you come across a man who is not thirsty? Have you come across a man who is not miserable? Have you come across a man who is not unhappy? Have you come across a man who is content, needs no more, who is fulfilled, needs nothing else to be added to him?

If you have not come across such a man, that means every man is thirsty. But people have forgotten their thirst. It would be better to say they have suppressed their thirst because the thirst is dangerous. The thirst creates search and one has to seek, and one has to make effort, and one has to dig deep into oneself. People avoid their thirst.

One man, a few days before, came to me and said, "I don't want to come and listen to you, because I am afraid. I am afraid I may really become interested in you and in what you say. I will come one day, but not now. I have other things to do."

Have you thought that you may be avoiding your basic thirst?

Religion is a basic thirst. No man can become satisfied and fulfilled unless he attains to a religious consciousness. There is no other way to be fulfilled.

But people go on saying that there is no God. That may be just a defence, because once they prove to themselves there is no God, then there is no need to seek and search; then they can remain wherever they are. Then they can remain in their mud, and there is no need to seek the lotus.

That's why Jesus says:

If any man thirst,
let him come unto me, and drink.

Jesus is available. It has been always so. There are people
who have attained and who are available—and you are thirsty.
But this is the misery: that you deny—you deny such people
who can quench your thirst. You deny that they have anything;
you deny that there is any water in their well because you are
afraid.

The greatest fear in life is the fear of God, the fear of coming
close to God—because coming closer to God will mean coming
closer to the death of the ego. Coming closer to God will mean
going farther from yourself. Coming closer to God will mean
dropping, surrendering, disappearing.

The greatest fear in the world is that of God, because God is
both death to the ego and birth, a rebirth of consciousness. But
you don't know about the rebirth; you can only feel the death.
You are just like a small child who is just going to be born, is
in the womb. For nine months he has lived a certain life of com-
fort, convenience. In fact, never again will he be so comfortable.
The womb is so comfortable, so warm. He is without any
responsibility; he has not to go to work in the factory or office.
He simply receives everything ready-made—no worries, no
fears, no responsibilities, no anxieties. He simply rests, sleeps
twenty-four hours.

And then suddenly comes the moment when he has to be
born. The child becomes afraid, because the child can only see
that this life is going to be destroyed—the life that he has been
living for these nine months. He cannot see a different life—a
life of open sky and air and sun, a tremendous opportunity to
grow. He cannot see. How can he see? He has no idea of it.

He can only see this: that the life he has been living is going to be destroyed. The birth to the child looks like death. He is afraid, he trembles, he doesn't want to get out of the womb.

The same happens again when you reach nearer to another rebirth of consciousness, where again you find another world—the world of God, called 'the kingdom of God'—of infinite light, of eternal beauty, of absolute truth. But you know *your* life: the life of the market, the life of the family, the house, the money, the ambition, the desire, the body—you know this. And moving towards God means going away from this. It looks like death. God is death, because God is rebirth also.

That's why Jesus says:

If any man thirst,
let him come unto me, and drink.

And the same I say unto you. If any man thirst, let him come unto me and drink, because yet a little while more am I with you. And then I go unto him that sent me. Remember, I am not repeating. I am not interested in commenting on Jesus. Through Jesus, I am again creating a situation which is absolutely new—or absolutely ancient, which is the same.

If any of you really feels thirsty, then the possibility is available. Don't miss it! And you can miss it. You can find a thousand and one excuses to miss it. Don't listen to those excuses; drop those excuses. Seek your thirst. If you are thirsty, then I am ready to become a well for you. The thirst can disappear, and only when your thirst disappears, for the first time you will feel what life is and its meaning—the beauty of it, the glory of it. Then life will become a decoded message to you. Up until now, you are carrying the seed. The message is there, but undeciphered.

Let me help you. If you are thirsty, don't try to escape from me. Let me help you.

10 Love is fragile like a flower. Hatred is powerful like a sword.

Will you please explain to me the Lord's Prayer, as given by Jesus?

MEDITATION CAN BE EXPLAINED, prayer never. It can be understood, but it cannot be explained. Prayer is something of the heart, very elusive, very indefinable. You can feel it, but you cannot think it. That is part of its nature. It is like love. It is not a technique.

Meditation is a technique. Prayer is not a technique. Meditation you can do: prayer you cannot do. You can only be prayerful. It has nothing to do with words: what you say in prayer is meaningless. How you say it, the space from where it arises, is meaningful—not the words.

Prayer is a gratitude, a deep thankfulness towards the whole, that you are here, that you are glad to be. It is against complaint. When you complain, you say you are miserable to be; when you pray, whether you say it or not, you mean that you are glad to be, you are thankful that you are. And Jesus' prayer is tremendously beautiful. No other prayer is so beautiful. Vedas have prayers, but they come from very sophisticated minds, and whenever a prayer comes from a sophisticated mind, it loses much. It becomes very refined, meaningful: and that's why it loses all meaning.

Jesus' prayer is almost childish. That's the beauty of it, the glory of it. If you want to understand Gayatri, the prayer in the Vedas, much can be said about it. It is a very condensed understanding; it is like a scientific formula; it is like Einstein's formula: $E=MC^2$. Much can be said about it, thousands upon thousands of pages can be written about it.

Jesus' prayer is not a scientific formula, it is just an outpouring of a simple heart; a child talking to his father—simple, very simple, it cannot be more simple than that. So, if you talk to Hindus, they will say, "What type of prayer is this?" If you talk to Buddhists, they will laugh, because they have very refined prayers, very cultured, sophisticated, philosophical, speculative, saying much in them.

Jesus' prayer does not say anything; it is simply an outpouring of the heart, as a lover talks to his beloved, or a child talks to his father. Let me repeat it: please don't ask for explanations; do it, and you will understand it.

*O*ur Father, who art in heaven, hallowed be thy name. Thy kingdom come. Thy will be done on earth as it is in heaven. Give us this day our daily bread. And forgive us our trespasses, as we forgive those who trespass against us. Lead us not into temptation, but deliver us from evil. For thine is the kingdom, the power and the glory, for ever and ever. Amen.

·⁕·

If I can truly experience the music of the fluteplayer,
can that be on the same level as the experience you
wish to occur with you? I am thinking of the Sufis:
I see, but I do not see. I am behind a glass wall.

The object is irrelevant. Only the subjectivity is relevant. Whether listening to me, or listening to a fluteplayer, or listening to the birds in the morning, or sitting by the side of the waterfall and listening to it, the same experience can happen. It happens not from what you listen to, it happens because you listen. Just listening gives you total silence; in deep listening you disappear. The whole art is how to listen.

Once you know how to listen, in deep receptivity, sensitivity, you are not there. The listener is not there, only listening. And when the listener is not there, there is no ego: there is no one who listens, only listening. And then it penetrates to the very core of your being.

If you listen to me with mind, you will miss. If you listen to the waterfall without mind, you will get. It is not a question of listening to me; it is a question somewhere concerned with you, with the listener. What I am saying is irrelevant; who is saying it is irrelevant. The whole thing is: are you surrounded by a deep silence? Have you become non-existent in that moment? Do you find suddenly that you are not, that you are a deep emptiness, throbbing with life, full, but empty, a tremendous silence, with not a single ripple of thought? Only then do you attain to a plane where truth can penetrate you.

So try to be a listener. Just hearing is not enough. Hear, you can; listening will need great discipline. It is the greatest discipline there is. If you listen, you are already delivered; because in that listening, suddenly you find yourself.

This looks like a paradox. You disappear, I say, and in that disappearance you find yourself. You are empty, and in that emptiness arises a fullness, a fulfilment. No thought is there.

And then there is understanding. And love flows, like breathing
—it goes in, it goes out, it goes in, it goes out. Then you start
sharing your being with the existence that surrounds you. Then
the part is no more part and separate—it throbs with the whole.
You fall in line with the whole, you are no more out of step. A
harmony has arisen—the celestial music, the music of the stars.

Then suddenly you are open. From every dimension God
flows into you. But the whole thing is how to be so receptive
and silent. Just now it can happen, just now it is happening to
many. I am not here; you are not there: and suddenly the meeting, suddenly the being.

What can you do? Because all doing will be a disturbance.
Whatsoever you do will bring you in from the back door;
whatsoever you do will be an effort and a disturbance. Don't
do anything; just be.

The whole art of religion is nothing but this—just be, allow,
be in a let-go; sitting by the side of the tree, just sit—nothing
else is needed, just sitting. Buddha attained to truth just by sitting
under the Bodhi Tree. Walking, just walk. Loving, just love.
Being, just be. By and by you start feeling that within you the
fragments are disappearing, and an integration is arising. By
and by it happens; by and by you start feeling that something
is penetrating you from the unknown, from the beyond. You
feel happy. You feel like a pregnant woman: the unknown has
entered you. You don't know who has come to your womb,
you have not seen the face yet, but you can feel the weight, you
can feel the unknown kicking in your womb. You know the
unknown has penetrated you.

Then you walk more carefully, you sit more carefully, because you have to protect. The unknown has become your
guest. You have to think and care about him, because the unknown is growing every day. The child grows and the mother
disappears. One day, only the child is and the mother is gone.
Mother means the past, and child means the present. Mother

means you as you are, and the child means you as you should be.

Nothing can be done specifically. You have just to create a climate around you of waiting, contentment, acceptance, delight, silence. You start already as if you have attained.

Listen to me again: you start already walking as if you have attained. It will be 'as if' only in the beginning: by and by, the 'as if' disappears. Walk like a Buddha, look like a Christ, delight like a Krishna. In the beginning it is going to be just 'as if'. But that 'as if' is not going to stay long, because you are really that which you are trying to act.

The whole thing is as if you go to Jesus, not knowing that he is Jesus, and he also does not know that he is Jesus; and you tell him that you are going to stage a drama and, "You look like Jesus. Would you please come and act as Jesus in it?" He agrees, and he comes to act. Of course it is 'as if' in the beginning, because he does not know that he is Jesus. You don't know that he is Jesus; he only looks like, appears to be. And then he starts playing in the drama and, by and by, the 'as if' disappears because he is. By and by the reality takes possession, and suddenly it erupts, and he is no more acting. He is simply being himself.

This is the case with you. You look like God. I tell you: act like God! And sooner or later you will discover that just by acting, you have discovered the reality. Because in reality you are already that; only you have forgotten it. So, if you start acting, the forgotten-ness will disappear. You will start remembering.

So, when you sit under a tree, sit like a Buddha. And don't be afraid, and don't be shy. Who is hindering you? And if you can sit like a Buddha, then why settle for less? When you play a flute, forget about yourself, play it like a Krishna. And I say to you: you are Krishna! And the flute is the same! Just you have to remember, and once you remember, immediately you will see the transformation—that now the song is not coming from you, it is coming from the beyond: you are no more in the way.

I have heard about Michaelangelo, that he used to use a device while working on his art pieces. Sometimes it would get dark; evening would come, and he would have to use candles. He would put the candles in a cup, because if you don't put candles in a cup, then your own shadow falls between you and your work, and it creates a disturbance. So he would put the candles into a cup—then the cup protects; then his own shadow would not come between himself and his work, and he would not be disturbed.

This is what is happening to you. Your own shadow is coming between you and your reality. The day you realize that it is only a shadow, then there is no problem.

One of the greatest thinkers of the West, Jean-Paul Sartre, has a certain theory. It may not be absolutely true; it is not. But it moves in the right direction. Even for wrong reasons he moves in the right direction. He says that there are two types of philosophies in the world: one, the philosophy of being; and another, the philosophy of doing. He himself thinks that he belongs to the second, the philosophy of doing, because he says, "Being in itself is nothing." Unless you do something, how can you be? When you paint, you become a painter; when you sing, you become a singer; when you dance, you become a dancer. If you don't do anything, who are you? All identity is lost—you become empty, you are no more there. So, he says, do something; because only by doing will you be something.

Buddha belongs to the first philosophy. He says: just be. Realize, without doing, who you are. Buddha is perfectly right, but Sartre is not perfectly wrong. And I can feel that what Sartre is saying can lead to what Buddha is saying. It can become a technique.

Act like a Jesus, and suddenly, your being is revealed. That being can be known without action also; but then it is more difficult, almost impossible, because you don't know where to look for a mirror. Without a mirror you cannot see your face. The face is there; you know it is there, but you cannot see without a mirror. The doing can become a mirror, and in the mirror the being can be revealed. Once it is revealed, you can forget about the mirror; you can throw the mirror away—there is no need for it.

Walk like a Jesus, sit like a Buddha, play on the flute like a Krishna, and by and by you will come to realize that it was not just an acting. You have stumbled upon something real. Your own shadow is no more falling—the clarity is attained.

When listening to me, sit like a Buddha, silent, receptive, feminine. That's why Buddha looks so feminine—have you watched?—no moustache, no beard, and the face of a woman. The meaning is, when you sit silently, your feminine part comes up, surfaces. When you act, your male part comes up, the feminine recedes. When you do something, your male part comes up. When you are in a non-doing, your feminine comes up.

Buddha attained to God through the feminine—in fact there is no other way to attain. The ultimate has to be attained only when you become a womb, a receptivity. Then it makes no difference.

Just sit and listen to the breeze passing through the pines, and you will find me there; or listen to me with no thought in the mind, and you will find the breeze passing through the pines. It is one and the same. But the whole depends on your listening—the quality of your listening is the question, not what you listen to.

I feel very identified with my mother. I tend to judge
her as harshly as I judge myself, and blame her for
my negativity. Can you talk about the nature of the
mother-daughter relationship?

This is a new disease created by the psychoanalysts in the West.
In a way it is very old and ancient, a very old trick of the mind.
But the garb that psychoanalysis has given it is very modern.

The human mind always tends to throw the responsibility
on to somebody else. Then you are freed of it. In the old days
people used to throw the responsibility on to God, fate, kismet
—a thousand and one words they had found. Then they were
no more responsible; then they were unburdened.

But this unburdening is very dangerous, because once you
feel that you are not responsible, then all doors for transformation are closed—because to feel responsible is the very basic
requirement for transformation. If I am not responsible for
what I am, how can I be responsible for any transformation?
If it happens, it happens; if it doesn't happen, it doesn't happen;
and if God is responsible, then he is responsible also for my
change, or no change. Then you start feeling that you are just
a puppet, and then you go on dragging yourself in the mud; then
your whole life becomes driftwood.

Don't think that this is a let-go. Let-go is a very alive thing.
This is dead wood, driftwood—it is not alive at all. A fatalist is
not alive at all, because he has thrown away all responsibility.
In throwing away responsibility he has also thrown away his
soul—he is no more a soul. The more responsible you feel, the
more authentic is the soul you have. Responsibility is your soul.

But those were old days, now we have forgotten about them.
Then came Marx: following Hegel, he created the same old
pattern again. He called it historic necessity: history is responsible,
not you. Economics is responsible, not you. Social structure is
responsible, not you—the old fatalism just garbed in new words.

Then came Freud. And he said if a child is not loved by the mother, then when he is grown up he will not be able to love: the mother is responsible. If the mother was negative, then the child will be negative: the mother is responsible. Freud was a Jew, and must have suffered from a Jewish mother; so the whole thing is thrown on to the mother. Now the mother becomes the God, the fate; and the whole thing seems to be absurd. Because if you ask who has made the mother this way, then her mother is responsible. Then go on and on. Finally you have to fall back on God: that's why I say the logic is the same. God is the mother of the whole, the original source from where everything comes.

You are destroyed by your mother. She is destroyed by her mother. Her mother is destroyed by hers, and go on and on and on. Finally you will have to fall back on God. This is the old trick, the old argument, just put in modern language.

But the whole trick is to throw away responsibility. Psychoanalysis stopped Western consciousness from growth. Psychoanalysis has not been a treatment; it is the illness. And the sooner the West gets rid of psychoanalysis the better. Because once you think that you are not responsible, you start living a life of irresponsibility. And nobody can say that you have to change. How can you change?

This question is from Nisha. I know her: she is negative. She is a miser. Her whole consciousness is constipated, closed; but a beautiful possibility, hidden. The bud has not opened, but once it opens there is going to be a beautiful flower in the world.

Now the problem is: if she feels herself responsible, then she has to do something immediately. If the mother is responsible, then what can she do? Unless the mother changes, which is not possible—that means unless the past changes, the present cannot change. But how can you change the past? It has already happened; it cannot be undone; there is no way. Then you accept the closed state of your consciousness, and you feel helpless.

The whole point of your being here with me is that you can do something. So try to understand my standpoint. Man's consciousness is absolute freedom. If you are negative, you have continuously to take the decision to remain negative. How the negativity was created is irrelevant, it is meaningless. It has happened; it is a given fact now, that you are negative, that you don't have any positive flowing energy. You have just a closing energy, which closes up on you, caves in upon you; and you have no door to move out from. The sky is lost, and you live in a dark cave.

It is irrelevant how it happened: there is no need to go into the past. I am telling you this is the foundation of Eastern esoteric psychology, that a man, whatsoever he is, has continuously to decide to be that way—only then can he remain that way.

It is like pedalling a cycle. You are pedalling a bicycle—you have pedalled for miles, but if you want to continue the journey you have to go on pedalling. If you stop pedalling, the bicycle is going to stop. Maybe through past momentum it may go on a little, a furlong or two at the most. But it is going to stop. And there is no need to go into research on how you started pedalling in the first place, because that is an absurd research. You cannot go into that, because go on and on and you cannot find the beginning. The past is eternity; you cannot find the beginning, and the whole search will stop your growth.

I tell you: you just stop pedalling, and the bicycle is going to stop. If you are negative, you are pedalling negativity continuously. If you take the decision just this moment not to pedal any more . . . your mother, or God—nobody is there to prevent you. It is your decision. But if you don't want to take the decision, then you can find a thousand and one excuses. Freud gives you a very wonderful excuse, very scientific-looking. But don't be deceived by the appearance. Freud has created a new myth. It is not science yet; in fact, the science of human consciousness is impossible, because the science is possible only in the world of cause and effect. And human consciousness is freedom; it has no cause and effect chain—science cannot be created in it.

*R*eligion is not science; it cannot be. More or less, religion is an art. It has no causality in it. So if you feel negative, that means somehow or other, knowingly or unknowingly, you have invested much in your negativity. Now you want to cling to it; you don't want to drop it. If you are miserly, you want to cling to it; you don't want to drop it. See the point. If you want to drop it, I say to you, "Immediately! This very moment!" Nobody is blocking the path. But you don't want to drop it; and you don't want to realize the fact that you don't want. Then you play a trick. You say, "I want to drop it, but how can I? My mother gave me the whole negative attitude towards life." So you hate yourself for being negative, and you hate your mother because she has made you that way. Nobody has made you that way, nobody is responsible.

Don't play these games. You are responsible. It may look like a burden I am putting on you. But if you look deeply, you will feel that this is the only possibility for your freedom. If you are responsible, only then can you be free. If others are responsible, how can you be free? If you are 'caused', you are 'caused' by others; then you can never be free, then you are just like a rock.

But I tell you: you are free. Your nature is freedom. That's why one word, *moksha*, does not exist in Western languages. There is no equivalent to it, no synonym for it: it means absolute freedom. The Eastern psychology is developed around the concept of *moksha*, absolute freedom. You can be free, because you are free. Realize this, this moment, and nobody is blocking the way—there is no barrier, no wall. But if you don't want to become free, don't think that you want to become free. People talk about freedom, but they want to remain in bondage, because bondage has its own comforts, securities, conveniences. Freedom is risky.

Miserliness has its own conveniences, otherwise nobody would be a miser. If you are not a miser, you become more insecure. If you cling to money, to things, you feel a certain security: at least there is something to cling to; you don't feel empty. Maybe you are full of rubbish; but at least something is there, you are not empty.

You go on clinging. With negativity you feel powerful. Whenever you say no, you feel powerful; the ego is enhanced. Whenever you say yes, you feel humble; the ego is destroyed. That's why you don't want to say yes, and you go on saying no. When you love, you become humble; when you are angry, you become powerful. Have you watched? When you are angry, you have four times more energy than you ordinarily have. In anger, in rage, you can throw a rock, a big rock. Ordinarily, if somebody tells you to, you cannot even push it, you cannot even move it. When you are angry, you have much power. When you are loving, all power disappears.

Can you find a more humble man than Jesus, more powerless than Jesus crucified? Just think of him. The people had gathered, the crowd was waiting: he would do some miracle—he will prove that he is powerful, that he is the son of God—this is the right moment and the right opportunity to prove it. But the crowd was very much disappointed. Nothing happened. Jesus simply prayed. Who had come to listen to the prayer? Jesus simply said, "Father, forgive these people, because they don't know what they are doing." He simply showed his love; and people had come to see his anger, people had come to see power. He will destroy everything; he will take over all power; he will become the high priest of the temple, or he will become the ruler of the country. He will become the King.

They had come to see power, and what they saw was just simple humbleness—a humble man, a poor man, crucified—

just praying. But that was the miracle. The greatest miracle that has ever happened on this earth happened that day. Being murdered and killed, he could still pray. That is the miracle. He could still pray for these people to be forgiven, because he knew they didn't know what they were doing; they were ignorant. "They are not doing, Father, knowingly; they are almost fast asleep, snoring. They are doing something unconsciously, so they are not responsible. Don't punish them."

This prayer was the miracle. This is where Jesus is, the heart of Jesus. But when you say no, you feel powerful; whenever you are angry, you feel powerful. Hatred is powerful, love is meek. And Jesus says, "Blessed are the meek." Blessed are the meek? Nobody wants to be meek. Hatred seems to be powerful. Have you watched two countries at war, how powerful they become when they are at war? Everybody is vibrant with power. When countries are at peace, the power disappears. When two persons love each other, the egos disappear; there is no power. Two persons in deep love are blessed, but they are meek, delicate. Love is fragile like a flower. Hatred is powerful like a sword.

So whenever you are negative, you feel powerful. And if you still want to feel powerful, you will cling to your negativity. Don't throw the responsibility on to your poor mother—because that is absurd. Take the responsibility on yourself, because that is the only chance of your transformation.

Look at the situation. And I am not saying, "Drop your negativity." I am simply saying, "Understand." If you want to carry it, it is up to you. Who am I to say to you, "Drop it"? If you are feeling good in it, I can simply bless you. Be blessed in your negativity. But then don't go on saying that you would like to drop it. Don't play this game. If you want to be negative, be negative. If you don't want to be negative, drop it. But this foolish game is not good: "I want to drop the negativity, but how can I?—because I was brought up in such a way that now it is impossible." Look. Observe. Be honest. The mother is not

the question. Your own honesty is the question, your own sincerity. And remember, I repeat again: I am not saying that
you drop it, I am not trying to save anybody—because how
can I save you against yourself? That's not possible.

I am simply trying to get you to see the fact of it. The very
fact delivers. That is the meaning of Jesus' saying 'truth liberates';
nothing else. Jesus cannot liberate you, neither can I. Truth
liberates. Just see the truth. If you want to be negative, if you
feel powerful through negativity, be negative and feel powerful.
But then don't try the opposite; then forget all about religion.
These people are mad—this Jesus and Buddha—their minds
are crazy. You are sane.

You simply remain in your sanity; follow negativity. If you
are honest, what will happen? If you are honest, you will see
that through your negativity you are creating a hell. Only you
are suffering, nobody else. Let the suffering come to such a point
where you cannot suffer any more; where you have to come out,
as if your house is on fire. Then you don't cling to it, you simply
run out; and you don't ask for the right way to get out. You
don't ask for a master: that you will have to learn the right way
and the right technique. Nobody bothers. You jump out of the
window; you run out of the back door. You find a way out
yourself, once you realize that the house is on fire.

*B*e true. Don't create deceptions around yourself. Don't
deceive yourself. And then, if you decide to be negative,
be negative; be perfectly negative. And I know that will help,
because it will create such a hell that you will have to come out
of it. Right now you go on creating hell, and you also go on
creating dreams of heaven.

Because of those dreams of heaven your hell is clouded;
you cannot see exactly what it is. It is as if the house is on fire,
and you are fast asleep, dreaming about a golden palace. Be-

cause of that dream you cannot see the house is on fire. So you go on dreaming about religion, transformation, growth, this and that, enlightenment. These are dreams, and because of these dreams you can't see the hell that you are continuously creating, continuously deciding upon, continuously helping. On one side you go on helping, and go on throwing fuel on the fire. And on the other hand you go on asking for methods how to get out of it.

Enough! Stop it! Look at the facts. If you want to live in hell, it is for you to decide; nobody else can interfere. Go into hell, but go totally; and that totality, that sincerity, will bring you out of it. Truth liberates.

My heart aches. Such a tiny crevice of it feels able to open to you. I want to melt and flow around you like a puddle; and I don't know how. Somehow my heart knows what it would feel like to open totally to you, and because it does not, it aches. And I shake and want to force, knowing that I can't. I love you such a tiny bit and it is beautiful.

This is from Anupama. I can see that her heart aches, but that heartache is beautiful. Remember: headache is always ugly, heartache is always beautiful. Headache comes when you think too much, you are obsessed with thinking. Heartache comes when you start feeling, when you start melting. Heartache is a good sign, a great indication that something is happening in your deepest core.

My heart aches. Such a tiny crevice of it feels able to open to you. Good. Help it to ache more; and don't try to avoid it, and don't try to get rid of it, because heartache is a positive thing. Headache is a negative thing. Headache is a disease; heartache comes only to those who are starting to be healthy and whole. Heartache is holy.

The word is the same: ache. That creates difficulty. Remember it, never forget it: whenever the heart aches, it shows that you are getting deeper into your being.

Love has its own ache. But blessed are those who attain to that ache of love. By and by the heartache will grow more and more. It will become intenser and intenser. Help it, so that it becomes a flame. You burn, but that burning is beautiful, because that fire will burn only the ego, not you. You will come out of it purified, like pure gold.

My heart aches. Such a tiny crevice of it feels able to open to you. Remember this too: that love never feels enough. Love always feels that it is not yet enough. That is a sign of love, it never feels enough. You can never feel enough love, you can never feel more than enough love. It is the very nature of love that it always feels that more is possible. "I can give more. I can flow more." Love is an infinity. So howsoever you open, you will always feel more is possible. It is a journey which begins, but never ends. Love's journey begins, but never ends. It is eternity.

I want to melt and flow around you like a puddle; and I don't know how. Nobody knows, nobody has ever known, nobody will ever know, because it is not part of knowledge. But you are already on the way; so move in the same direction. Allow it to ache more. Enjoy that ache. Delight in it, and help it. Don't fight it. Surrender to it. Don't stand aloof, don't be a watcher, don't separate yourself. Be drunk with it, get involved in it, be absorbed in it—so much so that only the heart aches and you are not there to watch and see. Only the heartache remains, and **you** have disappeared. Then it becomes a tremendous ecstasy. It is a birth pang; yes, a birth pain. One is reborn through it.

Somehow my heart knows what it would feel like to open totally to you. Yes, the heart knows, because heart has its own ways of knowing. They are not of the mind. It knows how it will be to be totally open. That knowledge is not something learned. That knowledge is inborn; that knowledge is carried like a blueprint in the heart. The day you come out of the original source—call it God's home—the day you are coming from the original source, that blueprint is put into your heart and sealed.

So, in a very strange way, you always know how it will feel to be totally open, to be totally flowing, to be totally in love and prayer. Yet you don't know, because the mind knows nothing about it. And yet you know, because the heart carries something in it which only needs flowering. It is like the seed which carries the blueprint of the whole tree. I say, of the whole tree. Even of a single leaf, the blueprint is there. There will be millions of leaves, but each single leaf has a blueprint hidden in the seed. The seed is very small, but it carries the whole plan, it carries the whole future in it.

The heart is the seed of God. It carries the whole plan in it. It carries your destiny, and your destiny is tremendously great. The seed may be very small, maybe a mustard seed. The smallness of the seed is not the point—don't be deceived by the smallness of it. It may just be atomic. It may not even be visible to the eyes, it may not even be visible to the greatest magnifying glass, it may be so tiny. It is very small—very small, atomic.

Nobody has known the atom, nobody has seen it yet. Only effects are known—it is an inference. Nobody has ever seen the heart—I am not talking about the physical heart. Nobody has seen the heart, the heart Jesus talks about, the heart Meera sings about, the heart Chaitanya dances about. Nobody has seen that heart yet; nobody is ever going to see it, because it is very, very small; it is invisible. But it carries God in it. It carries it, as every seed carries the tree.

Just look at a small seed—can you imagine what it can become? A tree can be born out of it, a great banyan tree, and then millions of seeds through this one seed. Scientists say that a single seed can fill the whole earth with greenery. A single seed can fill the whole universe with greenery, because there is no 'finitude' in it; it is infinite.

Each single heart can fill the whole universe. You will never be able to know what it is if you try to know through the mind. But if you relax into the heart, you will know in a very strange way. That is the way of the mystics, not of the intellectuals; that is the way of the poets, not of the philosophers. You will know it in a poetic way; you will know it, and it will never become knowledge. It will remain knowing, a groping; and it is beautiful, because whenever something becomes knowledge, it is already dead. Whenever you have known something, finished—then you are no more interested in it.

Love can never be known that way. It always remains unknown. It goes on alluring, it goes on invoking, it goes on calling you further and further. One peak, somehow, you reach; another peak is waiting. Another peak you reach; more doors open, more peaks are there waiting for you. It is an infinite journey. One knows, and yet one never knows.

My heart knows what it would feel like to open totally to you, and because it does not, it aches. And I shake and want to force, knowing that I can't. I understand. And you have observed your heart perfectly well. This is how it happens: you know nothing can be done, you know that doing will only disturb; yet you go on thinking, you go on wishing that something may be there, that something can be done—maybe, perhaps. And you know all the time nothing can be done, because it is not a question of doing. But still, the heart goes on feeling that perhaps there is a way.

One hangs, as if in a mist. But that is how one grows. Nothing can be done, and I know that nothing can also be done about the thinking that goes on thinking that maybe something can be done. Nothing can also be done about that. So accept that too; that too is part of the heartache. Accept whatsoever it is; and in total acceptance is transformation. You relax. Don't fight.

Remember, this is very delicate. Because whenever I say relax, you think now you are not to think; now you are not to do anything; now you are not even allowed to think about what to do. Then you have misunderstood me.

When I say relax, I mean relax; whatsoever goes on—let it go. I am not saying. . . . Because if you start thinking that let-go means that you are not to think about what is to be done, then you will start fighting with the idea which will be coming again and again. What to do?—you will start fighting with it. Let-go simply means no fight.

Now it becomes even more subtle. If fight arises, what will you do? Let go, let the fight be there. This is the delicate thing about it, that at whatsoever level you start fighting, drop fighting. Do you understand me? When I say 'drop fighting', don't *start* dropping it, because then you are not dropping, then you have started a new fight against fight.

It is tremendously significant. Let me repeat. I tell you not to fight, but fight arises. What will you do? Let it be. And I have been telling you not to fight, and fight arises. What should you do? Let it be. That is what I mean when I say don't fight—at whatsoever level struggle arises and you become concerned and you become separate from the on-going process—don't do that. Relax. Let it be, whatsoever it is. Accept whatsoever it is unconditionally, and by and by you will become aware that that is the only way to be, and the only way to be blissful, and the only way to be blessed. A totally different plenitude is attained when you relax.

. . . and because it does not, it aches. And I shake and want to force, knowing that I can't. Let it be so. Know that you can't . . . still it goes on: accept it.

I love you such a tiny bit, and it is beautiful. Love is beautiful, even a small window into the sky of love is beautiful. Of course, only a small part of the sky can be seen from the window, but it is still part of the sky. Sooner or later you will have to come out of the house; that which is beautiful will draw you. You will by and by be forced to come closer and closer to that which you love, that which is beautiful. Suddenly you will be running towards it; you will forget all about the house, the enclosure that you have been living in for lives together. Suddenly, in a deep ecstasy, you are out of the house, under the sky.

Only love can bring you out of your misery, only love can bring you out of your hell, because only in love can you forget yourself. And you are the misery, and you are the hell.

If you are not there, and there is no thought any more, how can you give such coherent and beautiful discourses? It seems like you are aware and understand what you are saying.

Such beautiful and coherent discourses are possible because I am not there. Once I am there, they will no more be beautiful. Not only that: they are beautiful because you are listening when you are not there. Once you are there they will no more be beautiful. The beauty exists only in an egoless space. You come, and ugliness follows.

If you are not there, and there is no thought any more . . . yes, I am not there, and there is no thought any more. That's why this river goes on flowing, because there is nobody to hinder it, nobody to obstruct it.

It seems like you are aware and understand what you are saying. It only seems. Don't be deceived by the appearance. I am not aware. I am drunk—drunk with awareness maybe, but I am drunk. But this drunkenness is called awareness. If your awareness is not also drunkenness, it is not awareness yet. If you are not drunk with awareness, you are not drunk yet. When awareness and drunkenness become almost synonymous, only then there is buddhahood, then there is enlightenment.

It seems like you are aware and understand what you are saying. It only seems: it is not so. I am drunk. And it seems that I understand what I am saying—I don't understand what I am saying; I am simply allowing it to be said. I am not trying to understand what I am saying, because that would be a duality; then I would be two—someone who is trying to understand what is being said. Then I would be in a dichotomy. And that's what happens when you say you are watching what you are saying all the time, whether you are saying it right or wrong. You are always trying to be consistent, logical, this and that. I am absolutely inconsistent. I am not trying in any way to understand what I am saying: I allow it. Because that is my understanding: that unless you allow, nothing of worth flows. If you try to say something which is meaningful, the meaning will be superficial. If you simply say it without any effort on your part, if you simply allow the divine, the whole, to flow through you, it is tremendously meaningful: the meaning is ultimate then.

And I would also like you not to try to understand what I am saying—because that is the only way to miss it, a perfect way to miss. If you want to miss what I am saying, try to understand. Just listen—there is no other need. It is a song to be heard, it is a dance to be watched.

I am a certain emptiness, and I would like you to participate in it. Be in rapport with me, don't try to understand; because then the intellect enters in, and then you are no more total. If you are total, whatsoever comes out is beautiful. If you are not total, at the most you can create an appearance of beauty, but it will not be beauty. Beauty is always of the total.

Please don't try to understand me—otherwise you will become a great knower, but you will miss knowing. Then you will become a rabbi, a pundit, a maulwi. But you will miss the real understanding that I am showering on you. Remember this: understanding is not needed—only a deep drunkenness, which is also awareness, is needed.

Be with me. When you are trying to understand, you are with yourself; you are trying to interpret me according to your mind, knowledge, information. According to your past you are trying to look at me; your eyes are clouded with dust, you will not be able to see me. Just be a mirror: reflect me; don't try to understand me. Echo me; don't try to understand me. And there will be understanding.

I have been so anxious to understand the mysteries of life that I have spent many years reading and learning whatever was available. All that I came to know is my ignorance. My question is this: Why, being so hungry of knowing, and at the same time so aware of lack of knowledge, have I never been able to find a single question after your lectures, even if I try, as I am trying now.

This is from Sugita. She is a professor; and she has been in search, and she has been honestly in search. She has read much, and she has gathered much knowledge. But knowledge can deceive you only if you are not an honest seeker. If you are a sincere seeker, knowledge cannot deceive you: you know this is all dust. That's why whatsoever she has been reading, studying, has not been able to deceive her.

All that I came to know is my ignorance. That is the beginning of knowledge, that is the beginning of wisdom. And because of it she is listening to me, not to understand: she is just drinking me, she is drunk with me, and no question is arising. Because if you listen to me in such a drunk state, you understand me totally —there is no gap, so questions cannot arise.

Remember: questions arise more out of your knowledge than out of you. If you know, and you think you know, then many questions arise. If you know that you don't know, then you simply listen. You are nourished by me, you drink me, you feel me. But there is no knowledge, so there is no struggle within you, no conflict within you: I immediately reach to your very heart. Questions do not arise, because you immediately understand.

When you listen through ignorance, understanding is total; when you listen through knowledge, there is no understanding, only chaos. Arguments arise, questions arise. There are two types of questions: one that comes out of ignorance—then it is beautiful; one that comes out of knowledge—then it is ugly and quarrelsome. But if your ignorance is total, then even that question which comes out of ignorance does not arise.

Sugita's ignorance is really total. She is a rare woman.

> *And ps: just because we were urged to create questions, I have made this one. But today's lecture gave me the answer. Before I ask you for water, you quench my thirst. But now a real question arose. Why, drinking and eating so much from you, am I still hungry and thirsty? But please do not answer it: I will just go on drinking and eating.*

If the question is really sincere, it will be answered even before you have asked it. Because then it is simply transferred to me; it is simply communicated non-verbally. When I come here, those who are really in tune with me immediately communicate whatsoever is their real question. They need not even ask, but the answer will be there. Because I am not speaking here in a vacuum, I am speaking to you.

That's why I don't like people who are not in deep
communion with me to be here—because they disturb; their
vibrations create clouds around here: then those who are in
tune with me cannot relate so easily. Even a single person who is
antagonistic here will not allow me to flow, will not allow me
to reach you. Those who are in tune with me need not ask.
Their very tuning . . . they may not even be aware of their
question, but the question has reached me. It is communicated.

And from that communication the answer is going to
arise. I am not there—just an emptiness to respond to you, just
a mirror to reflect you. And yet it is true that the more you
drink of me, the more thirsty you will feel—because a total
thirst is needed.

It has to be understood a little. I create thirst in you. I quench
it? and then I create more thirst in you. Because once the thirst
is total, then you will be able to drink out of God himself.
Then the master is not needed; then I become just a door.

So I will quench your thirst just to increase it more—so that
it becomes total; so that you are not there, only thirst throbbing
. . . only thirst, and only thirst. The disciple is not there, the
enquirer is not there. Then the master is not needed; then you
simply pass through me. I become the door.

So the master has to do two things: to create thirst; to quench
it just to create more. I go on pouring into you water and new
thirst; not only water, but thirst also. But each time your thirst
will be on a higher level, and each time your thirst will have
become more and more intense. Then a moment comes: you
disappear, and only thirst remains. When the thirst is totally
alone, and you are not there, then the master disappears. And
through the master, the God becomes available.

BOOK & CENTER LIST

- Just Like That
  (discourses on Sufi stories)

- TAO: The Three Treasures Vols I, II, III, IV
  (discourses on Lao Tzu)

- The True Sage
  (discourses on Hassidic stories)

- NIRVANA: The Last Nightmare
  (discourses on Zen stories)

- The Search
  (discourses on the ten Zen Bulls)

- Nothing To Lose But Your Head
  (a darshan diary)

- Hammer on the Rock
  (a darshan diary)

- Above All, Don't Wobble
  (a darshan diary)

- Come Follow Me Vols I, II, III, IV
  (discourses on the life of Jesus)

- Dang Dang, Doko Dang
  (discourses on Zen)

- A Sudden Clash of Thunder
  (discourses on Zen)

- I am the Gate
  (talks based on questions)

- The Silent Explosion
  (talks based on questions)

- Dimensions beyond the Known
  (talks based on questions)

translations

- La Rivoluzione Interiore
  (Italian—published by Armenia Editore)

- Hu Meditation og Kosmic Orgasme
  (Danish—published by Borgens Forlag A/S)

Nothing to lose book list—MGN

- SHREE RAJNEESH ASHRAM, 17 Koregaon Park, Poona 411 001, India   Tel: 28127

- SAGAR DEEP, 52 Ridge Road, Malabar Hill, Bombay 400 006, India   Tel: 364783

- ANANDA, 29 East 28th Street, New York, N.Y. 10016, USA Tel: 212 686 3261

- NEELAMBER, Blackmore Lane, P.O. Box 143, East Islip, N.Y. 11730, USA   Tel: 516 581 0004

- ANAND TARU, 25 Harbell St., Lexington, Mass. 02173, USA

- BODHITARU, 7231 SW 62nd Place, Miami, Florida 33143, USA

- SATSANG, 887 North La Salle, Chicago, Illinois 60610, USA   Tel: 312 943 8561/8549

- GEETAM, Box 576, Highway 18, Lucerne Valley, California 92356, USA   Tel: 714 248 6163

- PARAS, P.O. Box 22174, San Francisco, California 94122, USA   Tel: 415 664 6600

- ARVIND, 1330 Renfrew St., Vancouver, B.C., Canada

- KALPTARU, Top Floor, 10a Belmont Street, London NW1, England Postal address: 28 Oak Village, London NW5 4QN, England   Tel: 01 267 8304

- NIRVANA, 82 Bell Street, London NW1, England Tel: 01 262 0991

- PREMTARU, Church Farm House, Field Dalling, Holt, Norfolk, England

- SURYODAYA, The Old Rectory, Gislingham, by Diss, Nr Eye, Suffolk, England

- TUSHITA, North Moreton, Didcot, Oxfordshire 119BA, England

- GOURISHANKAR, 9 Ravensdean Gardens, Penicuik, Midlothian, Scotland, UK   Tel: Penicuik 73034

- PRASTHAN, 21 Wilmot Road, Glasgow C13 1XL, Scotland, UK

- PREMPATTI, 45-390 Desmonts, France

- SHANTIDWEEP, 25 Avenue Pierre Premier de Serbie, Paris XVIe, France   Tel: 720 7930

- ANAND NIKETAN, Kobmagergade 43, 1150 Copenhagen K, Denmark

- ARIHANT, Via Cacciatori della Alpi 19, 20019 Settimo Milanese, Milano, Italy

- SATYAM, 15b, route de Loex, 1213 Onex, Switzerland   Tel: 93 19 46

- AMITABH, Prins Hendrikkade 151, Amsterdam, Holland   Tel: 231870

- PURVODAYA, D-8051 Margaretenreid Fongi-Hof, West Germany   Tel: 08764/426

- SHREYAS, 8 Munich 60, Raucheneggerstr. 4, West Germany

- ANAND LOK, 1 Berlin 61, Mehringdamm 61, West Germany, Postal address: 1 Berlin 61, Luckenwalderstr. 11, West Germany

- SHANTI SHILA, 56 Dona Magdalena Hemady St., New Manila, Quezon City, Philippines

- ANAND NEED, P.O. Box 72424, Nairobi, Kenya, East Africa

- PURNAM, Caixa Postale 1946, Porto Alegre, Rio G. do Sul, Brasil   Tel: 21888

- SHANTI NIKETAN, 10 Bayfield Road, Herne Bay, Auckland, New Zealand

- PRASAD, Tokyo-to, Suginami-ku, Nishiogi-Minami 3-15-3 IC Salon 3F, Japan